The Contemporary Reading Skills Program

FROM PICTURES TO PASSAGES

Building skills in reading comprehension

Jane L. Evanson

Benita Somerfield, Project Editor
Brian Schenk, Copy & Contributing Editor

Contemporary Books, Inc., 180 North Michigan Avenue, Chicago, Illinois 60601

Copyright © 1984, 1981, 1978 by Contemporary Books, Inc.
All rights reserved
Published by Contemporary Books, Inc.
180 North Michigan Avenue, Chicago, Illinois 60601
Manufactured in the United States of America
International Standard Book Number: 0-8092-8026-4

Published simultaneously in Canada by Beaverbooks, Ltd.
195 Allstate Parkway, Valleywood Business Park
Markham, Ontario L3R 4T8 Canada

CONTENTS

              Reading Skills Preview   *1*

     Unit I: Finding the Main Idea and Supporting Details   *19*

    Unit II: Following the Sequence of Time, Place, Ideas, Events   *29*

   Unit III: Making Inferences   *37*

   Unit IV: Vocabulary Skills—Using the Dictionary   *45*

    Unit V: Reading Selections   *59*

   Unit VI: Following Directions   *77*

  Unit VII: Seeing Relationships   *85*

 Unit VIII: Vocabulary Skills—Dividing Words into Syllables   *97*

   Unit IX: Reading Selections   *107*

    Unit X: Drawing Conclusions   *127*

   Unit XI: Understanding Figurative Language   *141*

  Unit XII: Interpreting Imagery   *155*

 Unit XIII: Reading Poetry   *167*

 Unit XIV: Vocabulary Skills—Recognizing Prefixes   *173*

              Reading Skills Review   *185*

              Dictionary of Words You Need to Know   *205*

To the student,

From Pictures to Passages is a very unique kind of reading comprehension skill builder. It is unique because everyone who worked on this book believes that you, the adult learner, already have many of the skills you need to understand and enjoy different types of reading materials. You learned those skills, over the years, to survive in the world. You use them when you listen to someone speak, watch television, drive somewhere you've never been before, or learn a new dance. In *From Pictures to Passages* we will show you how to take those survival skills and use them to build your reading ability.

The best way to work with this book is to go through it carefully, unit by unit. Be sure to use the skill charts after each skill inventory to measure your progress. Your progress will be gradual but very real.

From Pictures to Passages uses what you already know to help you know more.

READING SKILLS PREVIEW

DIRECTIONS: Read the following five selections. After each selection, there are a few questions. The questions will give you a preview of the skills you will practice in this book. Answer each question based on the information in the selection by circling the letter of the **best** answer.

    The definitions of the **Words You Need to Know**, which are listed before every selection, can be found in the **Dictionary** at the back of the book. Be sure that you know the definitions of these words before you begin reading a selection.

1

Words You Need to Know

entrance   remembered
mistake   experience

1 When Donna walked into the large entrance hall of the
2 GED Testing Center, she had a nervous feeling that this would
3 be the beginning of a new stage in her life. Of course, Donna
4 remembered, the real beginning was the sign in the grocery
5 store window that had caught her eye. That sentence, "A career
6 is a life experience—not a life sentence," had stuck in her mind.
7 It was that sign that led her to finding out more information
8 about the classes for adults.
9   "A life experience, huh!" Donna had thought. "Man, I've
10 had enough of this one! Up every morning at 5:00 A.M.; slave all
11 day in Pete's Diner; then home to fall into bed. What a drag!
12 This is a life sentence!
13   Donna thought back to the first night of school. How shaky
14 she had felt! It had been over ten years since she'd dropped out.
15 For days, she didn't say a word in class. What if she said the
16 wrong things? Or made a mistake? She felt much better when
17 she found out that some of the other people in the class felt the
18 same way. It wasn't just her.
19   The reading class wasn't difficult—it was almost fun.
20 Donna learned much faster that she thought she would. Soon
21 she was in the GED program. And today, just ten months later,
22 she was ready for her test—she hoped.

23 The clock on the wall brought her back from her thoughts.
24 Then she noticed Bobby Marino, one of the men from her GED
25 class, leaning against the wall. He smiled and said, "Hi. Are
26 you taking the test, too?"
27 Donna smiled. "Yes. I think we still have a few minutes
28 before we have to go upstairs."
29 Both Donna and Bobby wanted to take their minds off the
30 upcoming test, so they talked about themselves. They talked
31 madly until test time. Soon, they were like old friends.
32 "In high school," Bobby said, "I was just one of the
33 numbers. I guess I felt lost most of the time. So I dropped out."
34 "That's about how I felt when I quit," Donna said.
35 "I've got a good offer from my uncle in the grocery
36 business," said Bobby. "But he wants me to get my diploma.
37 I'm not sure it's what I want, but once I get that piece of paper,
38 I'll be able to choose."
39 As Donna approached the testing room, she realized that
40 she felt much better after talking to Bobby. It somehow made
41 her less nervous to know that, at that moment, she wasn't the
42 only one just starting a new life experience.

1. The best title for the story is
   (A) GED Testing
   (B) Adult Classes
   (C) A Life Sentence
   (D) Starting a Life Experience
   (E) What a Drag

2. Right before Donna took the GED test, she was
   (A) in a classroom
   (B) in the entrance hall
   (C) in the grocery store
   (D) working at Pete's Diner
   (E) at Bobby's house

3. In line 31, the word *madly* most nearly means
   (A) with anger
   (B) without hope
   (C) without joy
   (D) with fear
   (E) without stopping

4. Based on the information in the passage, the reader can conclude that
   (A) getting a second job is the only way to get ahead in life
   (B) deciding to go back to school usually takes a lot of thought
   (C) education can lead to more job opportunities
   (D) going to night school after working all day can be tiring
   (E) a diploma always leads to a new job

5. From the line, "Yes. I think we still have a few minutes before we have to go upstairs," the reader can infer that
   (A) the testing center is in a two-story building
   (B) coffee and doughnuts are being served upstairs during the break
   (C) the bride will come down the stairs
   (D) the test will be given upstairs
   (E) they must use the upstairs exit

2

Words You Need to Know

expression	refused
society	persisted
needlepoint	

1 Everyone was meeting at Ken and Nancy's that night. The
2 group of friends had first met as young married couples, and
3 now, twelve years later, they were still getting together every
4 Thursday night to have dinner, talk, and tell stories about their
5 children. The men bowled once a week at Al's Bowl-A-Drome,
6 and all the wives met that night to play cards. It was a crowd of
7 people who liked to enjoy themselves, and although things got
8 a bit loud after a few beers, everyone always had a good time.
9 That night Phil Masterson reached for another cup of
10 coffee and good-naturedly asked, "Hey, Kenny, how come you
11 didn't show up for bowling last week?"

The conversation stopped, and all eyes, including Nancy's, were turned on Kenny, whose face, by this time, showed that he was uncomfortable.

"It's personal; I'll tell you later."

Nancy's high-pitched voice rang out. "What do you mean later, we want to know right now. You never said anything to me about not going bowling."

"Please, Nancy, I'll explain it all later tonight. I just don't want to talk about it now."

The group refused to be put off, and they began to kid Kenny.

"What's happening, Kenny?" persisted Phil. "You belong to a secret society or something?"

"Hey, Kenny, tell us about it. We might want to go with you!"

Kenny looked up at his wife and friends. "All right, all right—if you insist. I didn't say anything because I wanted it to be a surprise. I've gone back to night school."

Ron smiled. "Hey, Kenny, that's terrific. What classes are you taking?"

Kenny took a deep breath and replied, "Well, I'm taking science and reading and . . ."

The end of the sentence hung in the air.

All in one voice the others shouted, "And what?"

Again Kenny look uncomfortable. "I'm taking needlepoint. I find it relaxing."

The surprised expressions on the faces around Kenny turned to grins, and finally there was a sea of laughter around him.

When everyone had stopped laughing, Nancy began to speak. "There's nothing wrong with that. I think it's great that my husband's gone back to school. Rosie Greer, the football player, does needlepoint, you know, and nobody laughs at him. Ken, I think it's wonderful, and I'm glad that you're back in school. She walked over and put an arm around his shoulder and gave him a hug.

Kenny beamed.

6   READING SKILLS PREVIEW

6. Two of the night courses Kenny takes in school are
   (A) math and needlepoint
   (B) science and math
   (C) needlepoint and English
   (D) math and reading
   (E) reading and science

7. Choose the sentence that best describes the message of the passage you have just read.
   (A) You should study what interests you.
   (B) A bowling club helps to keep a group of friends together.
   (C) Choosing to go back to school takes a lot of thought.
   (D) Needlepoint is enjoyed by men and women.
   (E) Old friends are the best friends.

8. Before Kenny explained *why* he had missed bowling, his friends
   (A) got a substitute for the time being
   (B) gave up on him as a member of the team
   (C) demanded an explanation
   (D) wondered but didn't say anything
   (E) teased him so he had to explain

9. The word *beamed* (line 48) most nearly means
   (A) looked surprised
   (B) stared at the ceiling
   (C) broke into smiles
   (D) roared with laughter
   (E) looked into the lights

10. When the author says, "the end of the sentence hung in the air . . ." (line 34), she means the speaker
    (A) lost his train of thought
    (B) had to catch his breath
    (C) didn't want to finish his sentence
    (D) was through talking
    (E) lost his voice

3

Words You Need to Know

flare-up	nourishment
acknowledge	anonymous
sponsor	organization
---

1 Most people can have a drink or two or more and nothing
2 unusual happens. There are, however, some people who cannot
3 take even one drink. If they do, a chemical imbalance in their
4 systems causes the flare-up of a medical problem called
5 alcoholism. These people are called alcoholics.
6 Alcoholics do not usually recognize the problem
7 immediately. They, like many others, drink to be friendly, to
8 have fun, or to release tension. They do not become aware of the
9 condition until the *need* for alcohol becomes so great that it
10 affects every aspect of their lives. By that time the person may
11 suffer from a condition known as a blackout. This means he or
12 she cannot remember what events took place during or after
13 drinking. Family and friends cannot always cope with a
14 problem drinker. They often refuse to recognize that the
15 alcoholic is ill, preferring to view him as someone who just
16 drinks too much.
17 There is no cure for alcoholism. There are ways, however,
18 in which the alcoholic can help himself. First, he must face the
19 problem and acknowledge the fact that he is an alcoholic. The
20 alcoholic can then take positive steps to work out the solution.
21 Doctors and health counselors can help. Special clinics are
22 available in hospitals. These provide the alcoholic with a place
23 to stay for rest, nourishment, and withdrawal from the use of
24 alcohol. This is generally called a "drying out" period. Using
25 medicine and giving the alcoholic a chance to talk with a
26 professional who deals with personal problems may help the
27 alcoholic stop drinking.
28 Another form of help for alcoholics can be found in a group
29 called Alcoholics Anonymous, or A.A. This is an organization
30 made up entirely of people who at one time or another have had

drinking problems. In local telephone directories, there is a number listed as Central Service under Alcoholics Anonymous. When a person calls the number and simply says, "I think I have a drinking problem," he or she will get help. One or two people from the group will come to that person's home to explain the services available for self-help. If the alcoholic wants to attend an A.A. meeting, he does not have to go alone. These same visitors will pick him up for the meeting. A person going to A.A. will be asked to work on the drinking problem one day at a time. The first goal of the organization is to get a person through 90 days without alcohol. When the three months are up, the newcomer is given a chance to tell his story to the group. The group is able to give him moral support because everyone in A.A. has had the experience of withdrawing from alcohol use at one time or another. Later, the new member can pick a sponsor, or person he likes from the group. This is usually someone who will serve as a good model to follow. The sponsor generally becomes a friend and gives support to the newcomer through the difficult days ahead.

Once the alcoholic recognizes the problem connected with his use of alcohol, he knows that it would be dangerous to his system to *ever* have another drink. Since alcoholism cannot be cured, alcoholics must work to stay away from drinking each and every day of their lives. The self-control required to stay away from liquor is very difficult to develop, but many people have kicked the alcohol habit with the help of A.A.

11. When a person first joins A.A., the goal of the organization is to get him or her through each day for a period of
    (A) one day
    (B) 3 days
    (C) 3 months
    (D) 3 years
    (E) 90 months

12. Based on this passage, the reader can conclude that
    (A) alcoholism can be cured
    (B) it's all right for alcoholics to have one drink
    (C) some members of A.A. have never had a drinking problem
    (D) help is available for alcoholics
    (E) it's easy to deal with a problem drinker

13. When a person accepts that he is an alcoholic, he knows that
    (A) drinking is a danger to his mind and body
    (B) he can stop drinking in 90 days
    (C) everybody has the problem
    (D) he can easily identify an alcoholic
    (E) he'll like everyone in A.A.

14. Read lines 40 to 49 and write down what a new member of A.A. does after 90 days of not drinking.

_____

_____

15. The word *blackout* (line 11) most nearly means
    (A) forgetting what happens while drinking
    (B) blocking out the past
    (C) pulling the shades
    (D) going to bed early
    (E) passing out

4

Words You Need to Know

desire   perish
suffice   destruction

FIRE AND ICE

1 Some say the world will end in fire,
2 Some say in ice,
3 From what I've tasted of desire
4 I hold with those who favor fire.
5 But if I had to perish twice,
6 I think I know enough of hate
7 To say that for destruction ice
8 is also great
9 and would suffice

Robert Frost

16. The most important figure of speech in this poem is a *metaphor* in which
    (A) fire is compared to hate and ice is compared to destruction
    (B) fire is compared to destruction and ice is compared to death
    (C) ice is compared to desire and fire is compared to death
    (D) ice is compared to hate and fire is compared to desire
    (E) ice is compared to hate and fire is compared to death

17. When the author ends the poem with, "and would suffice" (line 9), he wants it to sound
    (A) silly
    (B) understated
    (C) sad
    (D) powerful
    (E) angry

18. The relationship of *fire* and *ice* in this poem is one of
    (A) part-whole
    (B) order
    (C) time
    (D) comparison-contrast
    (E) cause-effect

19. When the speaker says, "I think I know enough of hate" (line 6), he lets you know that he has
    (A) experience
    (B) knowledge
    (C) patience
    (D) happiness
    (E) assurance

20. The word *hold* (line 4) most nearly means
    (A) agree
    (B) look
    (C) grasp
    (D) carry
    (E) plan

5

Words You Need to Know

rejected   revoked
suspended   defendant
learner's permit

Use the information in the paragraph below to fill in the application for a driver's license on the following page.

Donald K. Small wants to get his first driver's license in Massachusetts. He successfully completed the Massachusetts Driver Education course and has certificate number 126. He received his learner's permit in Boston on September 12, 1975. Don is 5 feet 9 inches tall, weighs 168 pounds, and has black hair and brown eyes. He lives with his wife and 4 children at 96 Westview Road, Boston, Massachusetts 02111. He has been working since age 16. Don was born on October 8, 1945, in Boston. His social security number is 012-34-5678. Don is in excellent health and has no criminal record.

READING SKILLS PREVIEW

LICENSE APPLICATION
REGISTRY OF MOTOR VEHICLES
100 Nashua St.   Boston, Mass. 02114
To Be Filed at Nearest Registry Office
YOU WILL NOT BE EXAMINED IF YOU ARE LATE
Appointment fee $3.00 to be filed with application

LICENSE NO.

CASH NO.

★REPORT with this application for examination **AT**

Fee rec'd		ret'd		
Date Exam'd		Examiner		Result

VISION	Right	Left	Both	Result
Without Glasses	20/	20/	20/	
With Glasses	20/	20/	20/	
FIELD				
COLOR TEST	Red	Green	Yellow	Result
Reading test				
Law test				
Road test				
Car used				
Reg. No.				
Removal				
Restriction				

Applicant must answer every question below in ink: *Clerk*

REQUIREMENT: a birth, baptismal or school certificate or other satisfactory evidence of age.

1. Date of birth: month...day.......................year.........
2. Place of birth: City or town..State...................
3. Height ....ft.................inches.   4. Weight.................lbs.........
5. Color of hair........................   6. Color of eyes....................   7. Sex.
8. Has an application for a license to operate motor vehicles ever been rejected in Massachusetts or any other state?.........Where?..............
8a. Have you ever been issued a Learner's Permit in Massachusetts?..............
    Date... Where issued?..............
9. Have you ever had a license to operate   Date
   in Massachusetts or any other state?................Where?.............of Exp.
   Has it ever been suspended or revoked?...........
   If so, why?...................................Has it been restored?................
10. If unlicensed in Massachusetts, has your RIGHT to operate ever been suspended here or in any other state? (answer "yes" or "no")....................
    Has it been restored?...............
11. Have you been a defendant in a criminal action or a juvenile session other than a parking violation in which you were not acquitted?................
    If so for what reason?..............
12. Have you successfully completed the Massachusetts Driver Education Course?............
12a. Certificate number ....
    OVER—   FOR OTHER IMPORTANT QUESTIONS TO BE ANSWERED   —OVER

License application. Additional questions to be carefully answered:-

13. Have you any physical disability?...............If so, what?..
14. Have you ever been treated for:
    A. Any mental disorder?...............If so, by what institution or doctor?..................
    B. Any heart disorder?...................................
    C. Epilepsy or fainting spells?.........................
       (If you have answered "yes" to any of the above questions, explain fully using separate sheet of paper if necessary)
15. PRINT Residential address: No......................St..................City, Town, State, Zip Code
              (If non-resident give legal address)

☛ In case the license herein applied for is issued, I hereby irrevocably appoint the Registrar of Motor Vehicles or his successor in office my attorney upon whom process against me may be served as provided in the General Law and agree that process so served, if I am notified of such service as provided therein, shall be of the same legal effect as if served on me personally and that the mailing by the registrar of a copy thereof to me at my last address as appearing on the registrar's records shall be sufficient notice to me of such service. (G. L., Ch. 90).

I, the undersigned, hereby apply for a license to operate motor vehicles and state that the statements herein are true to the best of my knowledge and belief.

FALSE STATEMENTS ARE PUNISHABLE BY FINE, IMPRISONMENT OR BOTH (Gen. Laws, Ch. 90, Sec. 24)

Signature must be full and legible (Write) ....
                            First Name   Middle Initial   Last Name
PRINT   Mail address: No...St.........................City or Town   Zip Code
            (Not place of employment)

PRINT NAME HERE .... Social Security No.........................

PARENTAL CONSENT To be filled out by the parent, guardian, or person standing in place of parent of the above applicant.
TO THE REGISTRAR: I hereby certify that I am a (Check One)   (False statements made under penalties of perjury.)

parent ...., guardian ...., person standing in place of parent................, of the above named applicant who is less than 18 years of age but not less than 16½ years of age, and that my consent is given as required by G. L., Chap. 90, Section 8 that said applicant may be granted a license to operate motor vehicles.

(Write) NAME.. ADDRESS..

I hereby certify that I examined the above named applicant and that he did successfully pass the prescribed examination.

....
Signature of Examiner
Badge #

FORM E-2. 500M-2-74-1189-091679

ANSWERS AND EXPLANATIONS—READING SKILLS PREVIEW

Finding the Main Idea

1. **(D)** is the correct answer. The passage is about Donna and Bobby, both of whom feel that their lives will change if they pass the GED test.

Following Sequence

2. **(B)** is the correct choice because it is stated in lines 1 and 2 that Donna was in the entrance hall right before taking the test.

Making Inferences About Word Meaning

3. **(E)** is the correct answer because Donna and Bobby talked without stopping until test time.

Drawing Conclusions

4. **(C)** is the best answer. Donna's reason for going back to school was to improve her job opportunities. Also, Bobby would have the chance to work with his uncle if he passed the GED test.

Making Inferences

5. **(D)** is the answer because the reader knows that Donna and Bobby are waiting to take the GED test. (A) is not the answer because the building could have more than two floors.

Finding Supporting Details

6. **(E)** is the correct answer. The details are presented in line 33.

Finding the Main Idea

7. **(A)** is the answer. The passage focuses on Ken's return to school and his embarrassment over taking needlepoint. The story points out that there is no reason for him to feel this way about something he enjoys.

14 READING SKILLS PREVIEW

Following Sequence

8. **(E)** is the answer. His friends teased him about his reasons for missing bowling, forcing him to explain where he had been.

Making Inferences About Word Meaning

9. **(C)** is the best answer. When his wife supported his decision to study needlepoint, Ken probably felt good. This eliminates (A) and (B). (D) is a reaction to something funny, and (E) wouldn't make sense within the context of the story.

Understanding Figurative Language

10. **(C)** is the correct answer because Kenny didn't want to tell about his needlepoint class. There is no support for (A) or (B) in the passage. (D) and (E) are incorrect since Ken continues to talk.

Finding Supporting Details

11. **(C)** is the correct answer. This supporting detail can be found in lines 40-41.

Drawing Conclusions

12. **(D)** is the only answer that can be supported by the information in the passage. Answer (A) is false according to lines 52-53; (B) is false according to lines 50-52; (C) is false according to lines 29-31; and (E) is false according to lines 13-16. Answer (D) is true according to the information given in lines 17-27, as well as all the information about how A.A. helps alcoholics.

Seeing Relationships

13. **(A)** is the correct answer, supported by lines 50-52. There is no information in the passage to support any of the other answers.

Following Directions

14. You should have written that (1) he is given a chance to tell his story, and (2) he chooses a sponsor.

Making Inferences About Word Meaning

15. **(A)** is the correct answer according to the information given in the sentence in lines 11-13: "...*means he or she cannot remember what events took place during or after drinking.*"

Understanding Figurative Language

16. **(D)** is the correct answer. Lines 3 and 4 pair desire and fire, and lines 6 and 7 pair hate and ice.

Making Inferences

17. **(B)** is the correct answer. The word *suffice* means *to be adequate or satisfactory*. When the poet says that ice would suffice to end the world, he is not being silly (A) since the statement is true, expressing sadness (C), nor do the words sound powerful (D) or angry (E). He is stating the situation with less force than he could; so he is understating the truth.

Seeing Relationships

18. **(D)** is the correct answer. The poet is contrasting the two most powerful human emotions (desire or love and hate) by using two opposite things in nature.

Making Inferences

19. **(A)** is the best answer. The poet is saying that he has experienced the hatred in the world.

Making Inferences About Word Meaning

20. **(A)** is the only answer that makes sense in the line.

To fill in the license application form, you need the skill of Following Directions. You should have filled out the application as shown on the next page.

16 READING SKILLS PREVIEW

LICENSE APPLICATION
REGISTRY OF MOTOR VEHICLES
100 Nashua St. Boston, Mass. 02114
To Be Filed at Nearest Registry Office
YOU WILL NOT BE EXAMINED IF YOU ARE LATE
Appointment fee $3.00 to be filed with application

LICENSE NO.

CASH NO.

★REPORT with this application for examination **AT**

Fee rec'd	ret'd
Date Exam'd	Examiner	Result

VISION	Right	Left	Both	Result
Without Glasses	20/20	20/20	20/20	
With Glasses	20/20	20/20	20/20	
FIELD				

COLOR TEST	Red	Green	Yellow	Result
Reading test				
Law test				
Road test				
Car used				
Reg. No.				
Removal				
Restriction				

Applicant must answer every question below in ink: *Clerk*

REQUIREMENT: a birth, baptismal or school certificate or other satisfactory evidence of age.

1. Date of birth: month **October** day **8** year **1945**
2. Place of birth: City or town **Boston** State **Massachusetts**
3. Height **5** ft. **9** inches. 4. Weight **168** lbs.
5. Color of hair **Black** 6. Color of eyes **Brown** 7. Sex **Male**
8. Has an application for a license to operate motor vehicles ever been rejected in Massachusetts or any other state? **No** Where?
8a. Have you ever been issued a Learner's Permit in Massachusetts? **Yes** Date **September 17, 1975** Where issued? **Boston**
9. Have you ever had a license to operate in Massachusetts or any other state? **No** Where? Date of Exp.
   Has it ever been suspended or revoked?
   If so, why? Has it been restored?
10. If unlicensed in Massachusetts, has your RIGHT to operate ever been suspended here or in any other state? (answer "yes" or "no") **No**
    Has it been restored?
11. Have you been a defendant in a criminal action or a juvenile session other than a parking violation in which you were not acquitted? **No**
    If so, for what reason?
12. Have you successfully completed the Massachusetts Driver Education Course? **Yes**
12a. Certificate number **126**
    OVER— FOR OTHER IMPORTANT QUESTIONS TO BE ANSWERED —OVER

License application. Additional questions to be carefully answered:-

13. Have you any physical disability? **No** If so, what?
14. Have you ever been treated for:
    A. Any mental disorder? **No** If so, by what institution or doctor?
    B. Any heart disorder? **No**
    C. Epilepsy or fainting spells? **No**
    (If you have answered "yes" to any of the above questions, explain fully using separate sheet of paper if necessary)
15. PRINT Residential address: No. **96** **Westview Road** St. **Boston, Massachusetts 02111** City, Town, State, Zip Code
    (If non-resident give legal address)

In case the license herein applied for is issued, I hereby irrevocably appoint the Registrar of Motor Vehicles or his successor in office my attorney upon whom process against me may be served as provided in the General Law and agree that process so served, if I am notified of such service as provided therein, shall be of the same legal effect as if served on me personally and that the mailing by the registrar of a copy thereof to me at my last address as appearing on the registrar's records shall be sufficient notice to me of such service. (G. L., Ch. 90).

I, the undersigned, hereby apply for a license to operate motor vehicles and state that the statements herein are true to the best of my knowledge and belief.

FALSE STATEMENTS ARE PUNISHABLE BY FINE, IMPRISONMENT OR BOTH (Gen. Laws, Ch. 90, Sec. 24)

Signature must be full and legible (Write) **Donald** **K.** **Small**
                                           First Name Middle Initial Last Name

PRINT Mail address: No. **96** **Westview Road** St. **Boston, Massachusetts 02111** City or Town Zip Code
(Not place of employment)

PRINT NAME HERE **Donald K. Small** Social Security No. **012-34-5678**

PARENTAL CONSENT To be filled out by the parent, guardian, or person standing in place of parent of the above applicant.
TO THE REGISTRAR: I hereby certify that I am a (Check One) (False statements made under penalties of perjury.)

parent ...., guardian ...., person standing in place of parent ...., of the above named applicant who is less than 18 years of age but not less than 16½ years of age, and that my consent is given as required by G. L., Chap. 90, Section 8 that said applicant may be granted a license to operate motor vehicles.

(Write) NAME ADDRESS

I hereby certify that I examined the above named applicant and that he did successfully pass the prescribed examination.

FORM E-2. 500M-2-74-1189-091679

Signature of Examiner

Badge #

READING SKILLS PREVIEW—EVALUATION CHART

In order to see how well you've done on the Reading Skills Preview, see which questions you got right and which ones you got wrong. Then check against the chart below to find out which, if any, types of questions gave you trouble.

Circle the numbers of the questions you got right in the chart below. Enter the number of right answers of each type and the total.

Reading Skill	Question Numbers	Number of Correct Answers	Study Pages
Finding the Main Idea	1, 7		19-26
Finding Supporting Details	6, 11		20-23
Drawing Conclusions	4, 12		127-131
Making Inferences	5, 17, 19		37-42
Following Sequence	2, 8		29-34
Seeing Relationships	13, 18		85-93
Making Inferences About Word Meaning	3, 9, 15, 20		173-181
Understanding Figurative Language	10, 16		141-150
Following Directions	14, license application		77-82

Total number of correct answers _____

UNIT I: FINDING THE MAIN IDEA AND SUPPORTING DETAILS

Look at the picture below. What do all the people in this picture have in common?

All of the people in the picture are working. *Work* is the **main idea** of the picture. Although the occupations and people are different, they are all unified by the main idea, work.

20 FINDING THE MAIN IDEA AND SUPPORTING DETAILS

To locate the main idea, you have to use clues or **supporting details.** What is the main idea of the picture below? What facts or details give you clues to the main idea?

All of the people in the picture have something in common. They are all playing musical instruments. The main idea of the picture is, therefore, musicians or music. The main idea is always found by finding supporting details.

FINDING THE MAIN IDEA AND SUPPORTING DETAILS 21

Now study the pictures below. Which pictures illustrate the main idea of grocery shopping? What facts or details support your choices?

You are correct if you chose pictures 1, 2, and 5. Picture 1 shows someone paying for groceries. Picture 2 shows someone writing a shopping list. And picture 5 shows a woman shopping. Pictures 3 and 4 show activities that may follow grocery shopping, but they are not really a part of the main idea.

22 FINDING THE MAIN IDEA AND SUPPORTING DETAILS

Locating the main idea of something you read requires the same skills you use to locate the main idea of a picture. Once you know the main idea of a reading selection, understanding the entire selection becomes much easier. The main idea is **what the writer is writing about** and **the important thing he said about it.** A writer can state the main idea anywhere in a reading selection.

Let's examine some paragraphs. Sometimes the main idea is found in the first sentence as in the paragraph below.

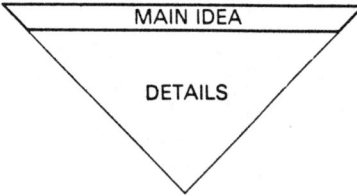

The past month has been a good one for Dave because of Ellen. She tutored him two nights a week. On September 29th, he passed his driving test—a real accomplishment! He's 38 years old and has never had a license. Ellen arranged for him to take the written test orally. He learned the entire driver's manual by listening to her read it and by listening to a tape. What a memory!

Exercise A

DIRECTIONS: Fill in the diagram below by writing the main idea in the space labeled main idea and writing each of the sentences that follow the main idea in the spaces labeled details. Notice how the details support the main idea about Dave's good month.

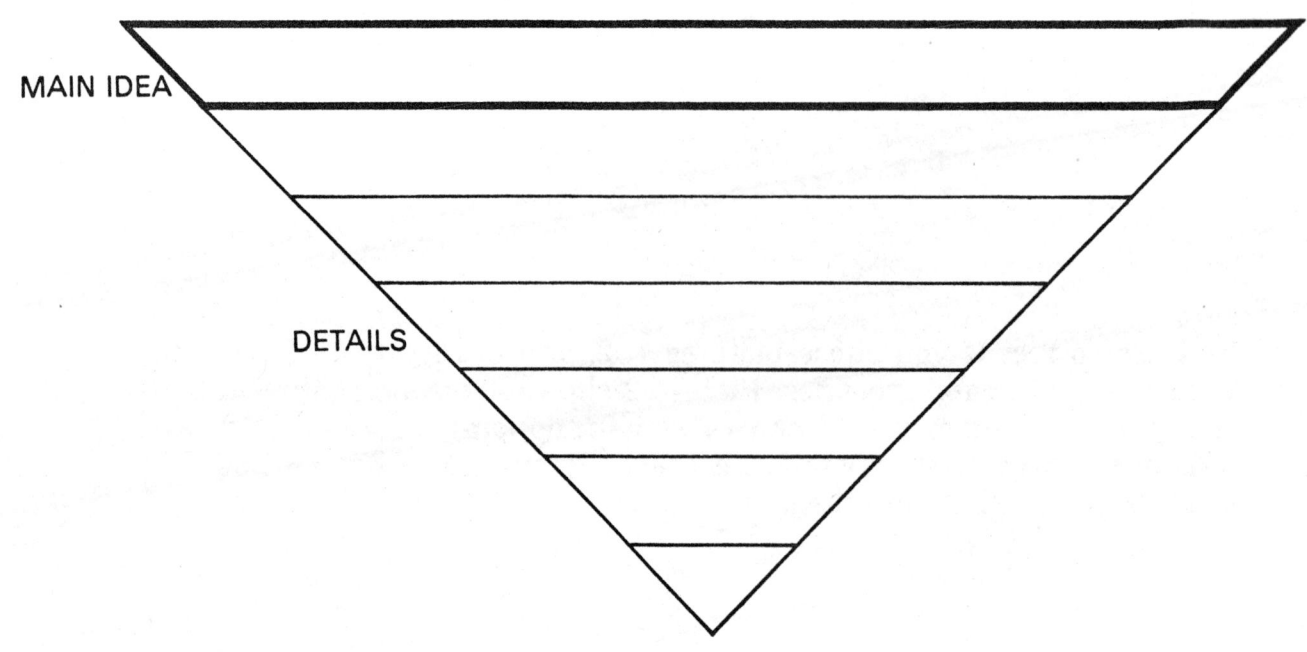

FINDING THE MAIN IDEA AND SUPPORTING DETAILS

The main idea is sometimes found in the last sentence as in the paragraph below.

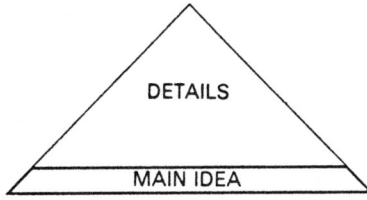

Sara has two sons and a daughter. Each morning she drops them off at a day-care center near her home. From there she catches a bus to work. Sara works in an office. She takes dictation from nine to twelve; then she types from one to five. She shops during her lunch break. After work she picks up her kids. After dinner her husband, Bill, takes care of the children while she goes to school. Sara is an active person.

Exercise B

DIRECTIONS: Fill in the diagram below by writing the first eight sentences in the spaces labeled details and writing the last sentence in the space labeled main idea. Notice how the details build to support the main idea that Sara is active.

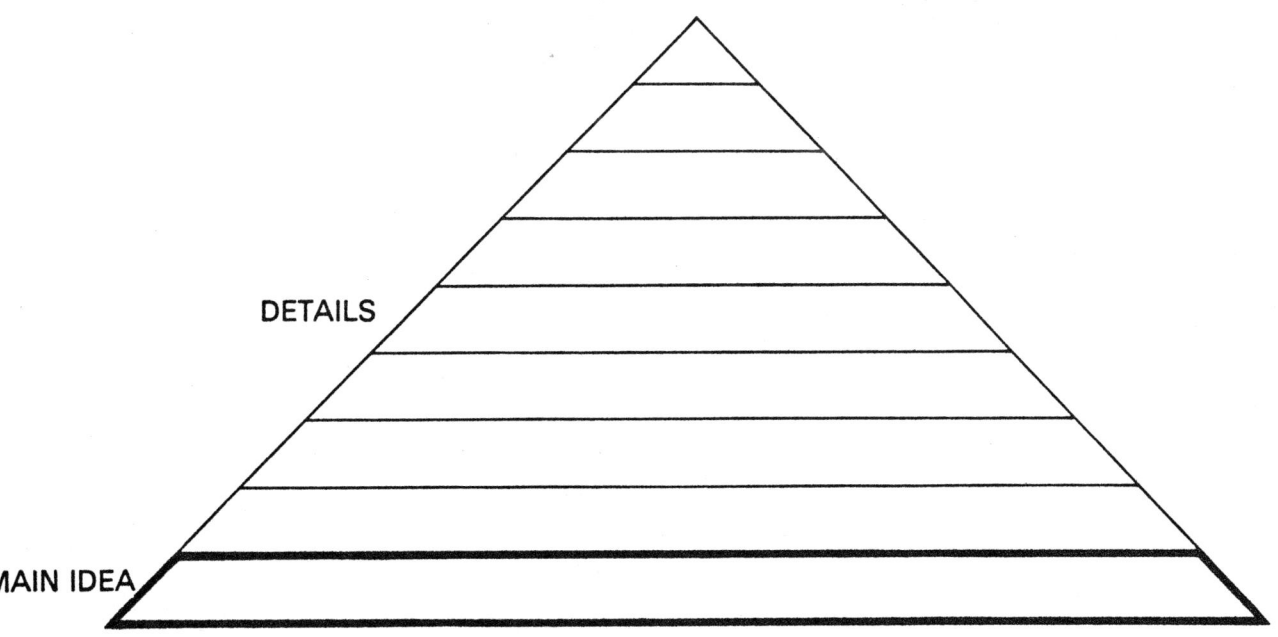

24 FINDING THE MAIN IDEA AND SUPPORTING DETAILS

Sometimes the main idea is found in the middle of the paragraph as it is in the paragraph below.

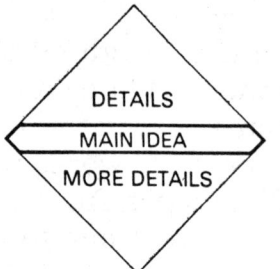

Bill usually sings in the car on his way to work. He often hums while working. Bill enjoys music. Sometimes during the lunch break, his friend plays the guitar while Bill sings. Another friend plays the harmonica.

Exercise C

DIRECTIONS: Write the five sentences of this paragraph in the five spaces in the diagram below, writing only one sentence in each blank. Notice which sentence is labeled main idea and which sentences are labeled details. Notice how the details are used to prove Bill's interest in music.

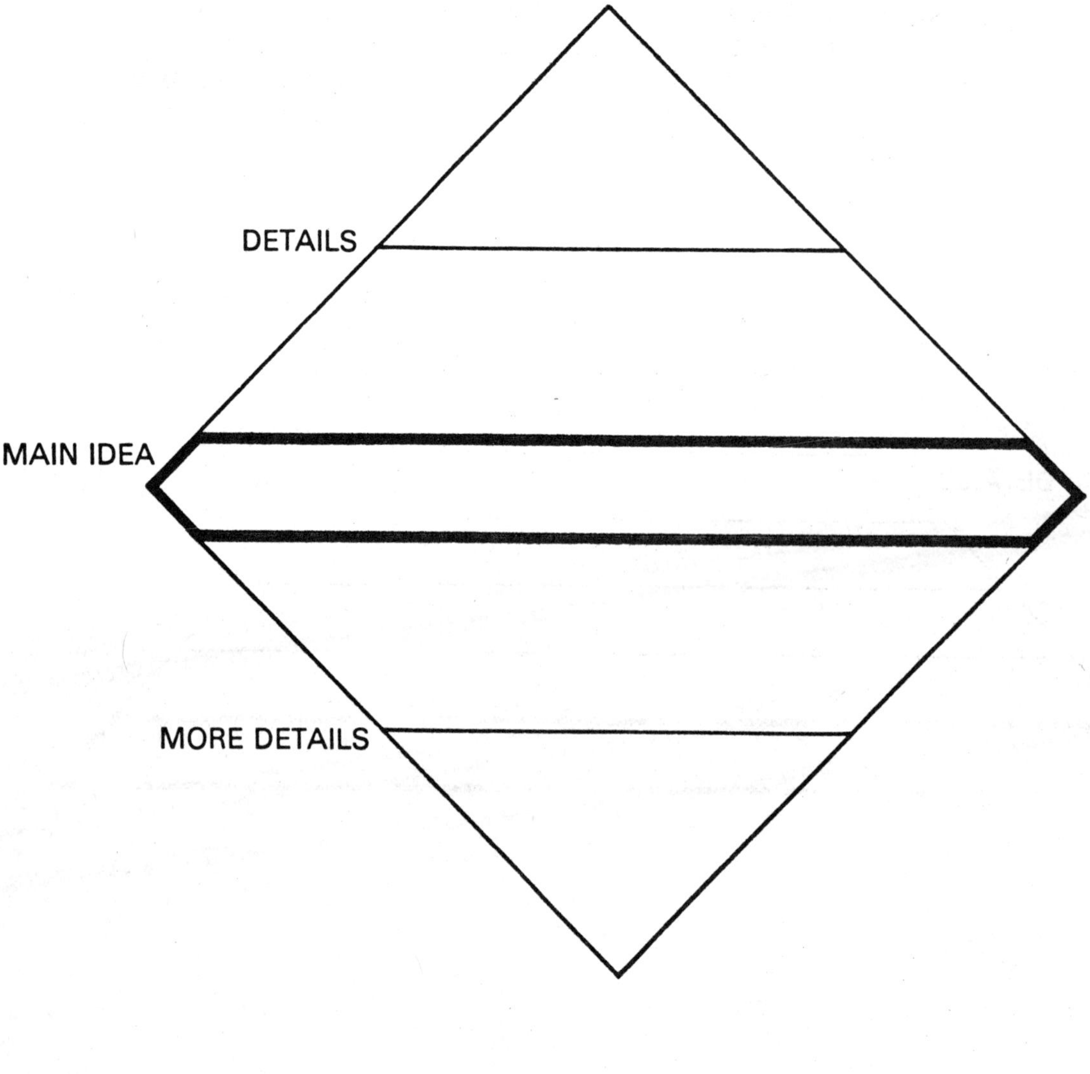

DETAILS

MAIN IDEA

MORE DETAILS

FINDING THE MAIN IDEA AND SUPPORTING DETAILS

Sometimes the writer doesn't come right out with the main idea. That is, the main idea is not directly stated. Then it is up to the reader to pull it together and mentally state the main idea for himself. The reader has to use all the sentences in the paragraph to **infer** or "guess" the main idea. Read the paragraph below and do the exercise that follows.

He was a nice guy. Or, at least that's what Jane had thought when she hitched a ride with him. There they were ten miles from nowhere when the man pulled to the side of the road. Now Jane had been in this type of situation before. But not with a stranger! And not in the middle of nowhere! As she thought about what she should do, the man moved a little closer to her.

Exercise D

DIRECTIONS: To help yourself figure out the main idea, write the sentences in the diagram below. The answer can be found in the Answer Key at the end of the chapter.

1 He was a _____
2 _____
3 _____
4 _____
5 _____
6 _____
7 _____

From these sentences you can infer that the main idea is:
1. Jane is crazy about the man.
2. The man wanted to be alone with Jane.
3. The man's car ran out of gas.
4. Don't hitch rides with strangers.

Exercise E

Now read the following short passage and pick the best title from the choices listed below. In order to pick the best title for the passage, you have to infer the main idea.

America is a nation of people who like to see records broken. No sooner is a record set for the most home runs, the highest jump, the fastest mile, the most pie eaten, or the most people to fit into a phone booth, than people eagerly wait for that record to be broken and a new record set.

Unfortunately, Americans break records that would be better off left unbroken, for example, the number of people killed in car accidents during long holiday weekends. The number goes up, and the record gets broken year after year. Some newscasters, like the man I heard last July 4th, seem to become so excited at the idea of breaking yet another record that they sound as if they're talking about a sports event.

"Last year at this time, two hundred people had been killed on our nation's highways. We're already up to three hundred right now! That's a 50% increase over last year's total! Our newsroom is predicting a total of 628 deaths before the weekend is over!"

I sometimes wonder why they watch and report the figures in this way. Am I being urged to get out there and pitch in to make this year a record-breaker too? One thing is certain. No one I know wants to be the star who breaks that record!

The best title for this passage is
1. Death on the Highway
2. Record-breakers
3. Dangers of Long Holiday Weekends
4. The Record No One Wants to Break
5. America's Favorite Pastime

FINDING THE MAIN IDEA AND SUPPORTING DETAILS 27

ANSWER KEY—UNIT I

Exercise A

MAIN IDEA: This past month has been a good one for Dave because of Ellen.

DETAILS:
- She tutored him two nights a week.
- On September 29th, he passed his driving test—a real accomplishment!
- He's 38 years old and has never had a license.
- Ellen arranged for him to take the written test orally.
- He learned the entire driver's manual by listening to her read it and by listening to tapes.
- What a memory!

Exercise B

DETAILS:
- Sara has two sons and a daughter.
- Each morning she drops them off at a day-care center near her home.
- From there she catches a bus to work.
- Sara works in an office.
- She takes dictation from nine to twelve; then she types from one to five.
- She shops during her lunch break.
- After work she picks up her kids.
- After dinner her husband, Bill, takes care of the children while she goes to school.

MAIN IDEA: Sara is an active person.

Exercise C

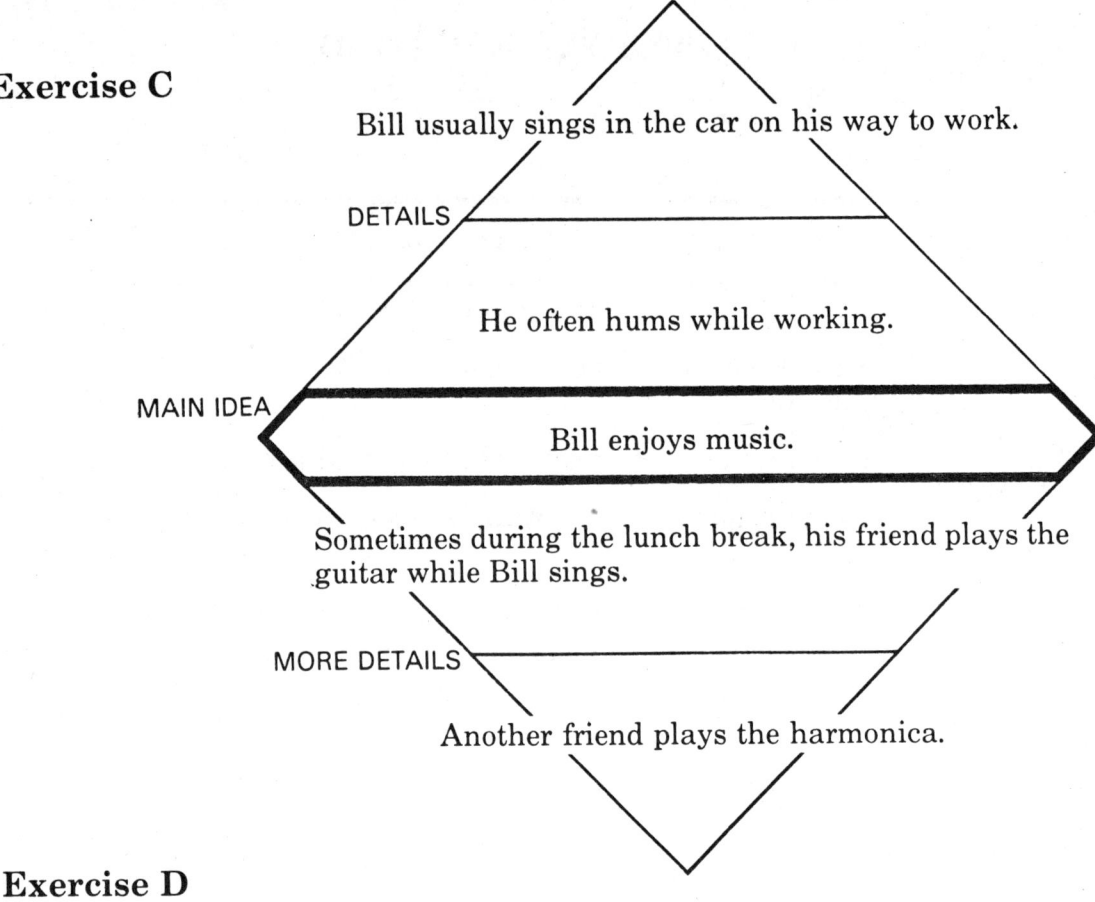

Exercise D

1. He was a nice guy.
2. Or, at least that's what Jane had thought when she hitched a ride with him.
3. There they were ten miles from nowhere when the man pulled to the side of the road.
4. Now Jane had been in this type of situation before.
5. But not with a stranger!
6. And not in the middle of nowhere!
7. As she thought about what she should do, the man moved a little closer to her.

None of the seven details support the ideas that *(1) Jane is crazy about the man;* or that *(3) the man's car ran out of gas.* Choice (2) describes the man's behavior accurately but is not the main idea of the whole paragraph. Of the answer choices, only (4) unifies all the supporting details.

Exercise E

Choice (4) is the best title for the passage. The other choices describe ideas in the passage, but do not include the point about record-breaking in this situation, a point that the author is trying to make.

UNIT II: FOLLOWING THE SEQUENCE OF TIME, PLACE, IDEAS, EVENTS

Here is one story.

Here is another.

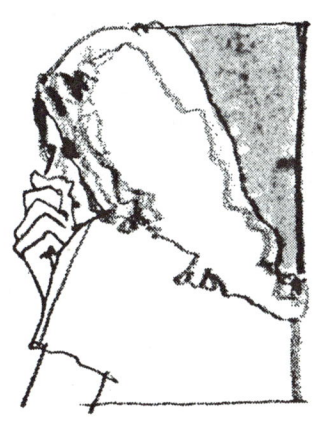  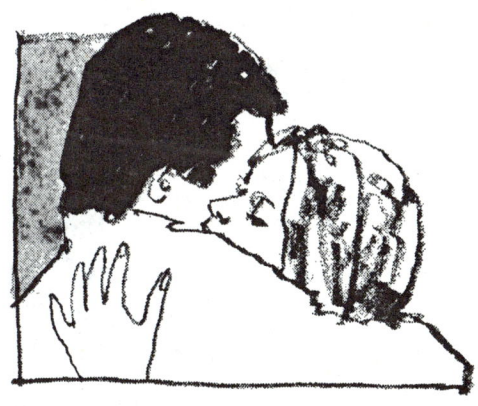

Whether these people end up as friends or enemies depends on the order in which the pictures appear. Just as the stories above depend on the order or placement of pictures, a written story depends on the order or placement of sentences.

30 FOLLOWING THE SEQUENCE OF TIME, PLACE, IDEAS, EVENTS

When events happen in logical order, these events are occurring in **sequence.** Each day, events follow each other so naturally in sequence that we hardly think about it.

You wake up, get out of bed, and brush your teeth in that sequence. You put your socks on your feet and your shoes on your feet in that sequence. You boil water, cook spaghetti, and eat it in that sequence. It would be impossible, uncomfortable, or silly to have these events happen out of sequence.

Exercise A

DIRECTIONS: Study the pictures below. Arrange them in logical order so that they tell a story. Number the pictures from 1 to 5, with picture number 1 being the event that happens first and picture 5 being the event that happens last. Correct answers can be found at the end of the unit.

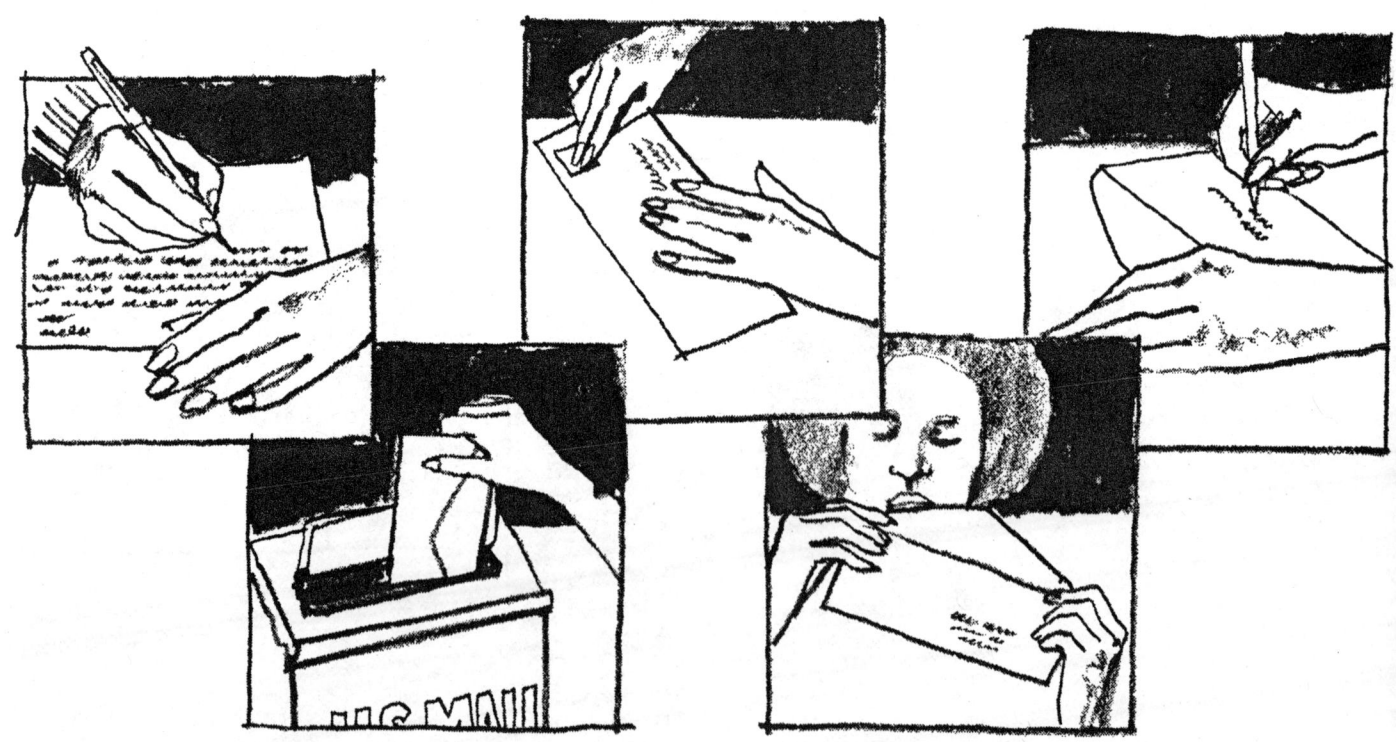

FOLLOWING THE SEQUENCE OF TIME, PLACE, IDEAS, EVENTS 31

Exercise B

DIRECTIONS: Follow the same directions as in Exercise A.

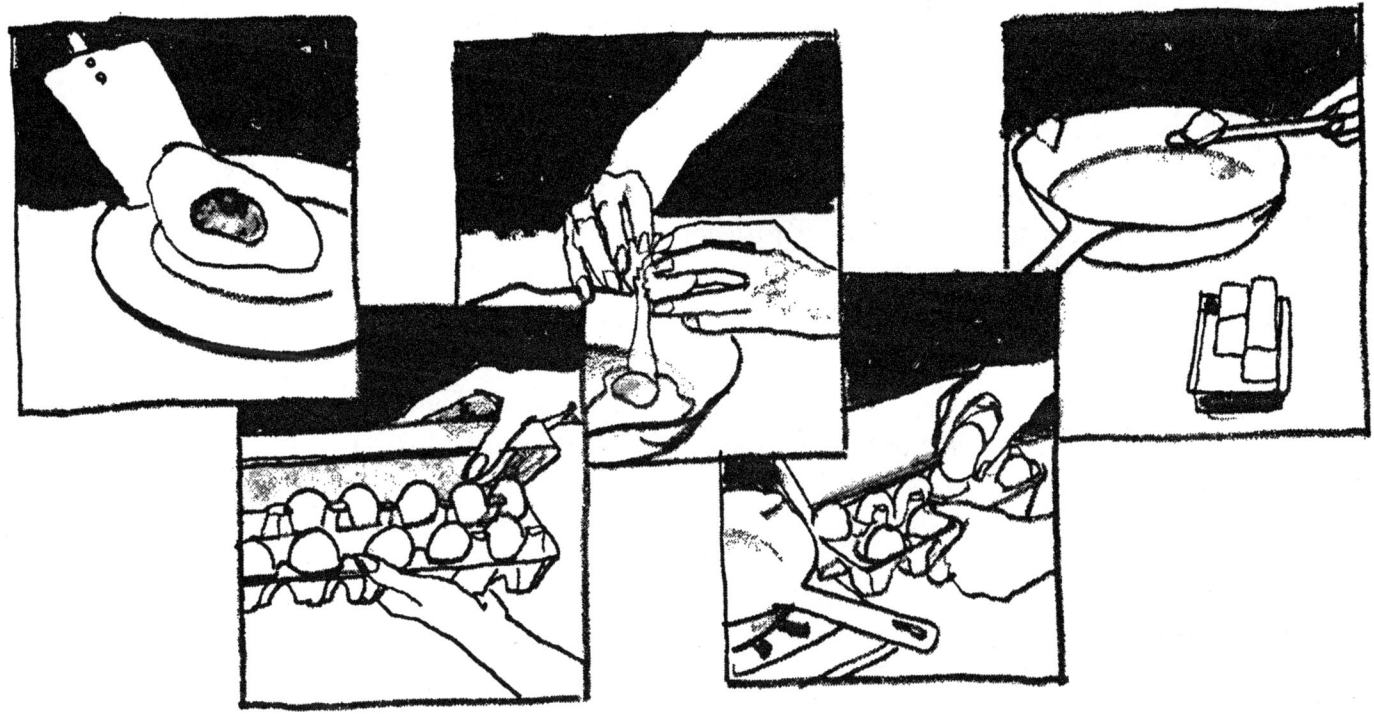

You are already familiar with some things that have a definite order or sequence. For example, numbers generally follow some definite sequence. When you count starting from the lowest number and going on to higher and higher numbers (as in 1, 2, 3, 4, 5), you are arranging the numbers in ascending (getting steadily bigger) order. When you count backwards (as in the *5, 4, 3, 2, 1, blast off* countdown), you are arranging the numbers in descending (getting steadily smaller) order.

Exercise C

DIRECTIONS: Arrange the following numbers in ascending order.

37, 29, 104, 14, 6, 8 ——, ——, ——, ——, ——, ——

Exercise D

DIRECTIONS: Count by sevens in ascending order.

7, ___, ___, ___, ___, ___, ___, ___, ___, 70

You also know that the letters of the alphabet are arranged in a definite sequence, called alphabetical order (*a* is always the first letter of the alphabet and *z* is always the last letter).

Exercise E

DIRECTIONS: Unscramble the following words. If you arrange the letters of each word in alphabetical order, you will find the word easily.

negbi _____

tofry _____

hilcly _____

tridy _____

pectac _____

When you write a sentence, you place the words in the sentences in the order that makes sense. If your reader is to understand what you want to say, you must follow certain rules of order called grammar.

Exercise F

DIRECTIONS: The following sentences do not make sense because the words are not in the correct order. Rearrange the words so that the sentences make sense.

1. checked should and by bite animal An be dangerous be may doctor a

_____

FOLLOWING THE SEQUENCE OF TIME, PLACE, IDEAS, EVENTS 33

2. the valve off turn and on the pilot light If lit stay not does your range gas, call company gas

   _____

3. cleaner drain chemical gloves avoid to rubber a Wear contact with

   _____

4. to a soda baking of paste Apply thick water and bite an insect

   _____

If you cook by using a recipe, you follow the steps of the recipe in a certain order. The sentences that give you the instructions on how to prepare the food are placed in the order in which you do the actual work. If you do not prepare the food in the proper sequence, you will not be making what the recipe intended.

Exercise G

DIRECTIONS: Number the steps in this recipe from 1 through 7, step 1 being the first thing you must do and step 7 being the last.

Apple Squares

_____ Place five pared, sliced apples on top of the batter.

_____ Sprinkle cinnamon and sugar on top of the apples.

_____ To the egg mixture, add vanilla, 1½ cups flour, 2 teaspoons baking powder, and a pinch of salt.

_____ Bake fifty minutes in a 350° oven.

_____ Cool and cut into squares.

_____ Mix 1½ cups shortening and 1 cup sugar together; add two eggs.

_____ Place this batter in a greased 9" × 13" pan.

34 FOLLOWING THE SEQUENCE OF TIME, PLACE, IDEAS, EVENTS

You should be able to look at a paragraph in the same way as a recipe. Each sentence should be in some order to give the reader the proper sequence in which things happened.

Exercise H

DIRECTIONS: Number the following sentences in the proper sequence, placing a 1 next to the sentence that describes what happened first and a 5 next to the sentence that describes what happened last.

_____ Thurgood Marshall was born in Baltimore, Maryland, in 1908.

_____ After he graduated from Lincoln University, he earned a law degree at Howard University in Washington.

_____ For the next 34 years he worked as a respected lawyer.

_____ After he graduated from high school, he went to Lincoln University in Pennsylvania.

_____ In 1967 he was named by President Johnson to be the first black member (Justice) of the Supreme Court.

Exercise I

DIRECTIONS: Follow the same directions given for Exercise H.

_____ Raphael doubled, getting Rico to third base.

_____ Willie got walked to first and the bases were loaded!

_____ Rico singled to first base with nobody out.

_____ When Lefty singled, he drove in Rico for the winning run.

FOLLOWING THE SEQUENCE OF TIME, PLACE, IDEAS, EVENTS

ANSWER KEY—UNIT II

Exercise A

Following is the correct order for the pictures in Exercise A:
1—writing the letter
2—addressing the envelope
3—sealing the envelope
4—putting a stamp on the envelope
5—mailing the letter

Exercise B

Following is the correct order for the pictures in Exercise B.
1—opening up the egg carton
2—melting butter or margarine in the frying pan
3—taking an egg out of the carton
4—breaking the egg in the frying pan
5—putting the cooked egg on a plate

Exercise C

6—8—14—29—37—104

Exercise D

7—14—21—28—35—42—49—56—63—70

Exercise E

begin, forty, chilly, dirty, accept

Exercise F

1. An animal bite may be dangerous and should be checked by a doctor.
2. If the pilot light on your gas range does not stay lit, turn off the valve and call the gas company.
3. Wear rubber gloves to avoid contact with a chemical drain cleaner.
4. Apply a thick paste of baking soda and water to an insect bite

Exercise G

Following is the correct order for the steps in the recipe:
4—5—2—6—7—1—3

1—Mix 1½ cups shortening and 1 cup sugar together; add two eggs.
2—To the egg mixture, add vanilla, 1½ cups flour, 2 teaspoons baking powder, and a pinch of salt.
3—Place this batter in a greased 9" × 13" pan.
4—Place five pared, sliced apples on top of the batter.
5—Sprinkle cinnamon and sugar on top of the apples.
6—Bake fifty minutes in a 350° oven.
7—Cool and cut into squares.

Exercise H

Following is the proper sequence for Exercise H.
1—3—4—2—5

1—Thurgood Marshall was born in Baltimore, Maryland, in 1908.
2—After he graduated from high school, he went to Lincoln University in Pennsylvania.
3—After he graduated from Lincoln University, he earned a law degree at Howard University in Washington.
4—For the next 34 years he worked as a respected lawyer.
5—In 1967 he was named by President Johnson to be the first Black member (Justice) of the Supreme Court.

Exercise I

Following is the proper sequence for Exercise I:
2—3—1—4

1—Rico singled to first base with nobody out.
2—Raphael doubled, getting Rico to third base.
3—Willie got walked to first and the bases were loaded!
4—When Lefty singled, he drove in Rico for the winning run.

UNIT III: MAKING INFERENCES

You walk into a room, and you see that your friend Mary is wearing a red dress. If you were asked the question, "What color dress is Mary wearing?" you would answer "red" immediately because you saw the dress. Sometimes, however, the answer to a question is not so obvious. Suppose that someone asked you how expensive the dress was. Then it is up to you to use whatever information you have about the cost of dresses that look like Mary's and come up with an answer. When you combine what you see with what you've learned throughout your life to answer a question, you are using the skill of **making inferences.**

Look at the pictures below. In order to answer the questions, you have to **make inferences.**

A. This man is at
   (A) a meeting
   (B) a party
   (C) his office

B. What has taken place?
   (A) a traffic jam
   (B) a race
   (C) an accident

C. This person is probably
   (A) hungry
   (B) tired
   (C) happy

38 MAKING INFERENCES

Let's compare notes. The man in Picture A appears to be enjoying himself at a party. The scene in Picture B shows an ambulance rushing somewhere. There has probably been an accident. In Picture C, the person is biting into a very thick sandwich. You can infer that she's hungry.

To answer these questions, you had to **make inferences.** You were using what you saw and read with what you've learned throughout your life.

Messages about what is going to take place come to us every day. Sometimes these messages are not stated directly. We get clues from things we *hear* and things we *see*. If the weatherman says, "Carry an umbrella today," you would **infer** that rain is expected. If your neighbor says, "You can't fight City Hall," you would **infer** that the situation he is describing is hopeless. If you see an unexpected raise in your paycheck, you can **infer** that the boss is happy with your work. Or, if you see cars jammed up on the highway to your home, you can **infer** that it will take you a while to get home.

Exercise A

DIRECTIONS: In the pictures below, study the expression on each face carefully. Then answer the questions that follow the pictures. Correct answers can be found in the Answer Key at the end of the unit.

1. Person #1 probably feels _____

2. Person #2 probably feels _____

3. Person #3 probably feels _____

In addition to making inferences from what we see and hear, we make inferences when we read. Writers don't always come right out with their messages. And, when they don't make direct statements, readers have to make inferences.

Exercise B

DIRECTIONS: Read the sentences below. Then infer how Ron feels. Circle the letter of the correct answer. Answers can be found in the Answer Key at the end of the unit.

1. Today Ron made the last payment on his car. Ron probably feels
    (A) upset
    (B) pleased
    (C) surprised

2. Ron had an argument with his boss. Ron probably feels
    (A) pleased
    (B) hungry
    (C) upset

3. Ron saw his grandchild for the first time. Ron probably feels
    (A) proud
    (B) disappointed
    (C) angry

4. Ron's best friend passed the GED. Ron probably feels
    (A) annoyed
    (B) sad
    (C) happy

5. Ron went fishing and caught three fish. Ron probably feels
    (A) disgusted
    (B) excited
    (C) unhappy

40 MAKING INFERENCES

Exercise C

DIRECTIONS: Read the following passages (Exercises C, D, and E) and answer the questions that follow. You will be asked to make inferences when you answer the questions. Put a ✓ next to your answer. There may be more than one correct inference that you can make about a passage. Answers can be found in the Answer Key at the end of the unit.

1 Car trips can really be fun if you have the right maps.
2 Some gas stations give away free maps. The maps show the
3 newest highways and can be used to help you figure out the
4 quickest routes. Even when you know where you are heading,
5 maps can add extra enjoyment to the trip. Finding small
6 towns, parks, and places with interesting names can help pass
7 the time. You may want to visit some places just to see what
8 they look like. Map reading is a skill itself. You'll learn to
9 judge road conditions, distances, and the sizes of towns. Using
10 a map to plan a trip can be as much fun for some people as the
   trip itself.

Some of the inferences that can be made about using road maps are:

____ using road maps may save time

____ road maps are entertaining

____ highways are hard to follow

____ you learn more about a trip by using a road map

____ you cannot travel without a road map

Exercise D

1 One of the most difficult things to figure out is the kind of
2 clothing that should be worn on a day when the temperature
3 may change sharply. Especially in the warm spring, summer,
4 and fall months, people like to enjoy the fresh air, and they

5 leave coats and sweaters at home. It is much wiser to carry an
6 extra layer of clothing, though. The surprising case of George
7 Mellow points out the danger of being unprepared. George's car
8 broke down on a sunny day in April. It was late in the day, but
9 he walked toward the nearest town to find a garage. On the
10 way, the temperature dropped from 62°F to 48°F, and he found
11 himself shivering. When he reached the town 90 minutes later,
12 he had to be taken to the local hospital. George was treated for
13 exposure. His failure to carry a coat cost him two days of
14 recovery in the hospital.

The reader should infer from this selection that extra clothing is helpful to have because:

____ weather reports are not very accurate

____ sharp changes in temperature affect the body

____ cars may break down at the wrong time

____ exposure may occur even when the air is above 32°F

____ people often die of exposure in the spring

Exercise E

1 All the bars are closed on election day. This wasn't always
2 the case. At one time politicians would buy rounds of drinks
3 and pay everyone in a bar to go over to the polls and vote. Of
4 course, they were told who to elect. That doesn't happen today
5 because state laws say that all bars must be closed the day of
6 the election.
7 Closing the bars didn't solve all of the voting problems.
8 Some people just don't care enough to vote for anyone. This, of
9 course, influences election results since, in a democracy, the
10 government is supposed to represent the people. Many excuses
11 are given by those who don't vote. Sometimes it's the weather
12 and sometimes it's the people running for office. People who
13 don't vote have a number of different reasons for not
14 participating in the democratic process.

42 MAKING INFERENCES

The feeling expressed by the author is that people who do not vote

___ help to elect the person of their choice

___ hurt the democratic process

___ have good reasons not to vote

___ do not like any of the people running for office

___ make up reasons for not voting

ANSWER KEY—UNIT III

Exercise A

1. Person #1 probably feels mischievous, playful, or perhaps she knows something you don't know.
2. Person #2 probably feels angry or very annoyed.
3. Person #3 probably feels worried, nervous, or in some way anxious.

Exercise B

1. **(B)** You can infer that to finish paying for a car will not make someone feel *surprised,* since most people keep track of payments, nor *upset,* since people generally feel good after paying off a debt.

2. **(C)** Arguments don't generally make people feel *pleased,* unless they win, and there is no evidence that Ron did. It is possible that some people feel *hungry* after an argument, but this is not a logical feeling to infer in the situation.

3. **(A)** There is no detail in sentence 3 that would support the inference that Ron was either *angry* or *disappointed* by his grandchild. The logical inference to make, based on most people's reactions to a first grandchild, is that Ron feels *proud.*

4. **(C)** There is no reason to infer that Ron had either of the negative reactions stated in (A) or (B). When his best friend passed the test, the logical inference to draw is that Ron felt pleased.

5. **(B)** People who go fishing are not generally *disgusted* or *unhappy* when they catch three fish, unless the fish are very small. There is no indication that these are small fish.

Exercise C

You should have chosen the following as correct inferences:

using road maps may save time (see line 3)
they are entertaining (see lines 4-6)
you learn more about the trip by using a road map (see lines 8-9)

44 MAKING INFERENCES

Exercise D

You should have chosen the following as correct inferences:

sharp changes in temperature affect the body (see lines 9–14)
exposure may occur even when the air is above 32°F (see lines 10–13)

Exercise E

You should have chosen the following as correct inferences:

hurt the democratic process (see lines 8–10)
make up reasons for not voting (see lines 10–14)

UNIT IV: VOCABULARY SKILLS— USING THE DICTIONARY

Knowing the meanings of the words you read is the key to understanding the meaning of a reading selection. If you come across a word that you don't know, when you are reading, you should use a dictionary to look it up. By using a dictionary, you can locate just about any word and its meaning. You can figure out how to pronounce it. You can find out about its origin (where it comes from). And you will find synonyms (words that have the same meaning) and antonyms (words that have the opposite meaning).

The words in the dictionary are arranged in alphabetical order. Exercises A through G will test how well you know the alphabet.

Exercise A

DIRECTIONS: Name the letter that comes just before the letter that is written below. Work as quickly as you can.

____ d ____ j ____ k ____ s

____ g ____ q ____ p ____ r

Exercise B

DIRECTIONS: Name the letter that comes just after the letter that is written below.

e ____ b ____ g ____ o ____

h ____ c ____ k ____ i ____

VOCABULARY SKILLS—USING THE DICTIONARY

Exercise C

DIRECTIONS: Arrange the words below in alphabetical order by numbering them from 1 to 8 in the spaces to the left of the words.

_____ plumber   _____ dollar

_____ baseball   _____ noise

_____ alimony   _____ check

_____ gasoline   _____ money

Exercise D

DIRECTIONS: For each of the following pairs of words, circle the word that comes first in the dictionary.

comb *or* capon

lift *or* laugh

money *or* mister

grandstand *or* gasoline

Exercise E

DIRECTIONS: Which word in each of the following groups, reading across, would come first, second, third, and fourth in the dictionary? Notice the *second* letter in each word. Arrange each row of words in alphabetical order by numbering them from 1 to 4 in the spaces to the left of the words.

1. _____ gossip   _____ grumble   _____ guard   _____ gloomy

2. _____ owner   _____ oven   _____ office   _____ opinion

3. _____ diploma   _____ dock   _____ deposit _____ damp

4. _____ point   _____ pilot   _____ person   _____ pinch

VOCABULARY SKILLS—USING THE DICTIONARY

Exercise F

DIRECTIONS: Arrange each of the following rows of words in alphabetical order by numbering them from 1 to 4 in the spaces to the left of the words. Notice the *third* and *fourth* letters of each word.

1. ____ balcony ____ basket ____ balloon ____ bald

2. ____ curious ____ cushion ____ custody ____ curtain

3. ____ plug ____ pleasure ____ pliers ____ plastic

If you look at any page in a dictionary, you will see two words at the top of the page in a darker and larger print. These are called guide words. The left-hand guide word is the first word on the page. The right-hand guide word is the last word on the page. All words that come after the first guide word alphabetically and before the last guide word are on this page.

Exercise G

DIRECTIONS: Underline the words below that would come between the guide words HUMOROUS and HURRY on a page in a dictionary.

hundred	hungry	hubcap
hydrant	horrible	hurdle
hunk	huddle	humble
humid	hunter	hurricane

Pronouncing the Word

When you find the word you are looking for, you will see its pronunciation next to it. A symbol is used for each sound, and the key to these symbols is usually found at the front or back of your dictionary. Use the key to figure out how to pronounce unfamiliar words.

Exercise H

DIRECTIONS: Below is a list of some common pronunciation symbols, followed by a word with that sound. Add the letters given in parentheses to either the beginning or end of each word to form your own word that has the same sound. Circle the letter or letters that represent that sound.

/ a /	at	_____ (fl)	/ z /	chose	_____ (n)
/ ā /	pain	_____ (S)	/ ī /	rival	_____ (ar)
/ i /	it	_____ (spl)	/ ī /	sty	_____ (le)
/ k /	cat	_____ (ch)	/ o /	off	_____ (ice)
/ e /	bet	_____ (ter)	/ ō /	oat	_____ (fl)
/ ē /	eat	_____ (m)	/ ū /	use	_____ (am)
/ u /	fun	_____ (ny)			

Understanding Word Origins

Some dictionaries include information about the origins of words. Many words in the English language came to us from other languages. For example, *kindergarten* is borrowed from the German language. It means "garden of little children." The word *tangerine*, a small tasty orange, originally came to us from Tangiers, Morocco. Some words in the English language come to us from people who were associated with that particular thing. For example, Braille, the name of the system that makes it possible for blind people to read by touching a series of raised dots, was invented by Louis Braille.

Exercise I

DIRECTIONS: Study the words below. Choose the correct word to fill in the blanks in this exercise.

> brunch
> umbrella
> good-bye
> breakfast
> gardenia
> America
> sideburns
> smog

1. In Italian, *umbra* means *shade* and *ella* means *little*. We get a little shade from an _____.

2. When you don't eat, it is called a *fast*. While you sleep, you don't eat. When you wake and eat your first meal of the day, it is called _____.

3. If the air is polluted with smoke and fog, this mixture is called _____.

4. When leaving each other, people used to wish each other well by saying, "God be with ye." Today, this expression has been shortened to _____.

5. Dr. Alexander Garden developed a flower that is sometimes used in corsages. This flower that was named after him is the _____.

6. A meal that takes the place of both breakfast and lunch is sometimes called _____.

7. The country known as _____ was named after *Amerigo* Vespucci.

8. General Ambrose Burnside had whiskers down to the middle of his cheeks. Other men liked this style and copied him. At first, these whiskers were called "burnsides." Now the word has been changed to _____.

Choosing the Definition That Fits

It is important to remember that the definition that you choose from a dictionary must make sense in the sentence in which the word appears. If you find that a word you've looked up has several different meanings, you will have to rely on the relationship among the words in the sentence in which it appears to help you choose the correct definition. For example, the word *fire* means one thing when it stands alone: "Fire! Fire!" And it means something else when used like this: "Because business is falling off, they will have to fire five workers in our plant." The only way to know which definition to use is to see which one best fits the sentence or general meaning of the paragraph.

Exercise J

DIRECTIONS: Look at the pictures below and on the next page. Each one illustrates a different meaning of the word *strike*. Five sentences using the word *strike* are listed to the right of the pictures. Write the letter of the picture that illustrates the definition of *strike* as it is used in the sentence.

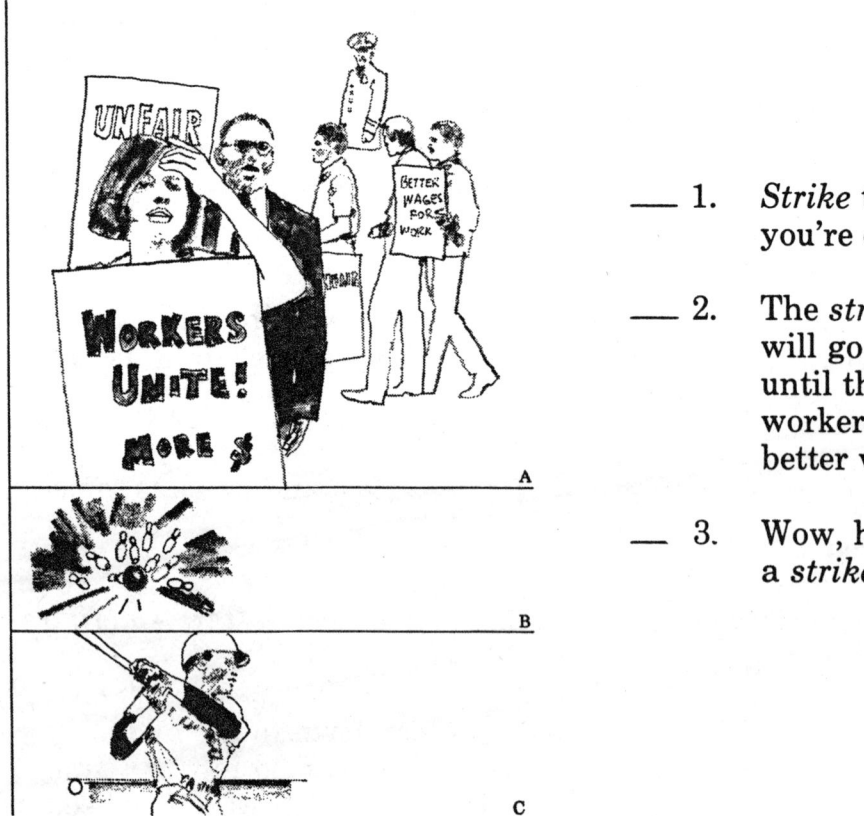

__ 1. *Strike* three—you're out!

__ 2. The *strike* will go on until the workers get better wages.

__ 3. Wow, he got a *strike!*

VOCABULARY SKILLS—USING THE DICTIONARY

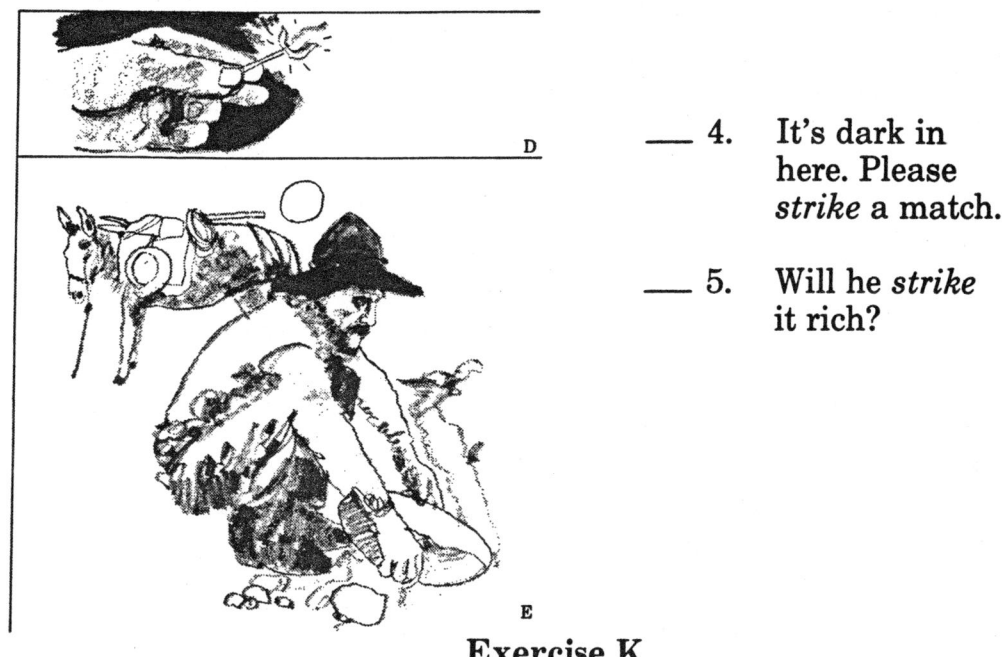

__ 4. It's dark in here. Please *strike* a match.

__ 5. Will he *strike* it rich?

Exercise K

DIRECTIONS: Now look up the definition of the underlined word in each sentence. Choose the meaning that fits the sentence. The meaning you want may not be the first definition given in the dictionary. Be careful, sometimes the definition you want is in the middle or listed last.

1. I needed another quarter to make a phone call.

    Definition: _____

2. Our living quarters were neat.

    Definition: _____

3. He is entitled to a fair trial.

    Definition: _____

4. Your work is fair, not excellent.

    Definition: _____

5. Livestock and farm produce are sold at the county fair.

    Definition: _____

6. Joe almost got stuck in that snow bank.

   Definition: _____

7. I went to the bank to deposit my paycheck.

   Definition: _____

8. Heart disease is the number one killer in the country.

   Definition: _____

9. Let's get right down to the heart of the matter.

   Definition: _____

10. I learned my part by heart.

    Definition: _____

11. This message comes from the heart.

    Definition: _____

Synonyms and Antonyms

If we use the same words over and over, a conversation can become dull. To liven up a conversation or written story you can use more specific, more interesting, or just different words.

Good is one word that is overused. It can usually be replaced with a word that will be more exact or more interesting.

> It was a good evening — delightful
>
> It was a good meal — delicious
>
> She is a good babysitter — reliable, capable
>
> The lake looks good — cool, clean

Delightful, delicious, reliable, capable, cool, clean, are all synonyms in certain situations for the word *good*. A synonym is a word that means nearly the same thing as another word.

VOCABULARY SKILLS—USING THE DICTIONARY

Exercise L

DIRECTIONS: Write synonyms for the following words. You may use a dictionary if you wish.

1. fertile _____
2. offensive _____
3. smear _____
4. clammy _____
5. glint _____
6. opinion _____
7. stern _____
8. irk _____

Exercise M

DIRECTIONS: Use your dictionary to write the synonym for the following underlined words.

1. The chorus line danced with amazing precision. _____

2. The pebble skimmed the surface of the lake. _____

3. My grandparents are saving money to take an excursion. _____

4. The rest room facilities do not seem very sanitary. _____

5. He squandered all his money. _____

6. How do you know that story is authentic? _____

7. Wheat was scarce and the price of flour went higher. _____

VOCABULARY SKILLS—USING THE DICTIONARY

Exercise N

DIRECTIONS: Antonyms are words that have the opposite meaning. Write antonyms for the following words.

1. lustrous _____
2. vivacious _____
3. foolish _____
4. contented _____
5. sanitary _____
6. sterile _____
7. vanish _____
8. cheerful _____
9. young _____
10. broken _____
11. rainy _____
12. general _____

VOCABULARY SKILLS—USING THE DICTIONARY

ANSWER KEY—UNIT IV

Exercise A

 c d   i j   j k   r s

 f g   p q   o p   q r

Exercise B

 e f   b c   g h   o p

 h i   c d   k l   i j

Exercise C

8	plumber	4	dollar
2	baseball	7	noise
1	alimony	3	check
5	gasoline	6	money

Exercise D

capon
laugh
mister
gasoline

Exercise E

1. 2 gossip   3 grumble   4 guard   1 gloomy

2. 4 owner   3 oven   1 office   2 opinion

3. 3 diploma   4 dock   2 deposit 1 damp

4. 4 point   2 pilot   1 person   3 pinch

VOCABULARY SKILLS—USING THE DICTIONARY

Exercise F

1. __1__ balcony   __4__ basket   __3__ balloon   __2__ bald

2. __1__ curious   __3__ cushion   __4__ custody   __2__ curtain

3. __4__ plug   __2__ pleasure   __3__ pliers   __1__ plastic

Exercise G

You should have circled the following words: hundred, hunk; hungry; hunter; hurdle; hurricane

Exercise H

flat   chosen
Spain   arrival
split   style
catch   office
better   float
meat   amuse
funny

Exercise I

1. umbrella
2. breakfast
3. smog
4. good-bye
5. gardenia
6. brunch
7. America
8. sideburns

VOCABULARY SKILLS—USING THE DICTIONARY

Exercise J

1. __C__
2. __A__
3. __B__
4. __D__
5. __E__

Exercise K

1. a coin having a value of twenty-five cents
2. a place of lodging or residence
3. impartial, honest, and free from prejudice
4. up to the average, satisfactory, passable
5. an exhibit of products (as of farm products), usually for prizes
6. any moundlike formation or mass
7. an institution for loaning, exchanging, housing, or issuing money
8. the central organ of the circulatory system
9. the core or central part of anything
10. so as to be perfectly memorized, by rote
11. the seat of the affections and emotions, as distinguished from the head

Exercise L

1. fruitful, rich, productive, inventive
2. foul, rotten, vulgar
3. spread, defame, slander
4. damp, cold
5. gleam, glitter
6. belief, decision, conviction, judgment
7. austere, grim, severe, strict
8. irritate, annoy

58 VOCABULARY SKILLS—USING THE DICTIONARY

Exercise M

1. accuracy, exactness
2. top, exterior part, face
3. journey, trip
4. healthy
5. wasted, spent extravagantly or foolishly
6. authoritative, trustworthy, reliable
7. rare, scanty, insufficient

Exercise N

1. dull
2. dead, dreary, lifeless, monotonous
3. wise
4. dissatisfied, unhappy
5. unhealthy
6. fertile
7. appear, arrive
8. unhappy, sad
9. old
10. repaired, fixed, whole
11. sunny, fair
12. specific, exact, precise

UNIT V: READING SELECTIONS

DIRECTIONS: Read the following five selections. After each selection, there are a few questions. The questions will give you a chance to review the skills you have practiced in Units I, II, and III. Answer each question based on the information in the selection by circling the letter of the **best** answer.

The definitions of the **Words You Need to Know** that are listed before every selection can be found in the **Dictionary** at the back of the book.

1

Words You Need to Know

license   requirements
permit   vary
regulations   vehicle

1   When a person applies for a driver's license, he/she must
2   meet certain requirements. First, one must get a learner's per-
3   mit. This is a form that may be obtained at a special office usu-
4   ally called "The Registry," officially known as The Registry of
5   Motor Vehicles.
6   The requirements for a learner's permit vary from state to
7   state. Usually, however, the learner's permit will be given to
8   persons sixteen and one-half years or older. A would-be driver
9   must also get some practical experience. He/she must learn
10 how to drive whatever vehicle or vehicles his license will cover.
11 In many places, high schools have driver education programs.
12 The benefit of going into this type of program is that one can
13 get experience for a small fee. This course teaches the rules and
14 regulations that a person must know in order to pass a written
15 test. Schools also provide experience in a special car that has
16 certain extra equipment. These cars have two sets of brakes.
17 This special dual-control equipment helps the teacher keep con-
18 trol of the car if the student driver makes a mistake. People who
19 go to a high school driver education course can sometimes get a
20 lower rate on their car insurance.

Some people get their driver education by going to a driving school. These schools are usually listed in the yellow pages of the telephone book or have ads in local newspapers. The school is a regular business that prepares people to pass driving tests. As a business, they charge a fee that might be as much as $85.00 or more. The cost covers the time spent in actual driving as well as in helping a student prepare for the written test.

Many people learn to drive by going out to practice with a relative or friend. People who do this are also required to have a learner's permit. There are certain drawbacks in learning to drive this way. For example, one should not try to learn to drive with anyone who gets nervous or angry. A nervous and angry teacher generally makes a nervous and angry student. Also, since regular cars do not come equipped with two sets of brakes, there is some amount of risk involved in learning to drive this way.

When a person gets a learner's permit, he also gets a booklet with questions and answers. These are the same questions used in the written examination. After the student driver has studied all the questions and actually learned how to drive, he/she will go to the Registry with the driving teacher or a friend. Usually one takes the test in the same car in which the practice took place because this is a familiar vehicle to operate. A questionnaire and form must be filled out first. The form is an application for a license. The questionnaire is the written test, and a person must know most of the answers in order to pass this part of the requirement. An eye test is also given. The student looks into the window of a machine and is asked to identify marks or letters. This tells the Registry that a person is able to see well. People who wear glasses must be sure to bring them to the test.

The road test is given by a special inspector. He is a person trained to check the ability of the driver. He sits in the front passenger seat and gives directions like, "Turn around on this hill," or "Take a left turn at the lights." When all the directions have been followed, the student drives back to the Registry office. Most people who do not get a license the first time will be told when to return to try again. They will also be told what rules of the road were not followed or what skills they lack so that they can practice.

1. According to the passage, in order to get a driver's license one must
   - (A) go to driving school
   - (B) own a car
   - (C) pass a written test
   - (D) practice driving with a relative
   - (E) have his picture taken

2. When a person wants to get his driver's license for the first time, step one would be
   - (A) get car insurance
   - (B) take an eye test
   - (C) pay $85.00
   - (D) go to driving school
   - (E) get a learner's permit

3. The best title for this selection is
   - (A) Red Light, Green Light
   - (B) A Visit to the Registry
   - (C) Safe Driving
   - (D) Getting a Driver's License
   - (E) Driving Can Be Fun

2

Words You Need to Know

buff	stagnant
development	shutter
jagged	productive

1 Paul Hamilton had never been to night school before, so
2 when he signed up for a course in photography, given nights at
3 Sloat High School, he wasn't sure of what to expect.

The teacher was Phil Downs, a real camera buff. He had learned about cameras in the army. The classroom filled quickly, and Phil called out the names for attendance.

"Jenny Morgan?"

"Right here."

"Paul Hamilton?"

"Here."

"Rose Lopez?"

"Yes, I'm present."

"Bill O'Neil?"

As Phil continued to call the roll, Paul looked around the room at the other students. It seemed to be a good group.

Paul looked forward to coming to class each week to hear about shutter speeds, timed exposures, and all the other facts of picture-taking to be learned. Soon he was off each weekend to take pictures around the city. It was strange to get up *deliberately* at 7:30 on a Saturday morning and walk up and down the streets looking for interesting subjects to photograph.

On this particular Saturday, Paul woke a half hour later than usual and decided to take his car to a nearby park that had a stagnant pond in the middle of it. As he pulled over to the side of the road, he noticed a woman having car trouble. "Excuse me," he said to the woman who was kneeling down by what appeared to be a flat tire. "Need some help?"

The woman stood up and smiled. "Aren't you Paul Hamilton? I'm Jenny Morgan from the photography class at the high school. I don't need any help, but you can keep me company while I change this flat."

Paul's face creased into a broad grin when he thought of this slim woman changing a flat tire.

Jenny explained how she'd come out to the park to take some pictures and had cut her tire on a jagged rock. They continued to talk as Jenny changed the flat. Finally, when she was finished, she wiped her hands on a handkerchief and asked, "Does your family mind you going out so early to take pictures?"

"Oh," he replied, "I live alone. How about you? Doesn't your old man mind being left alone on a Saturday?"

"No, I live alone, too."

They spent the entire day taking pictures in the park, pointing out interesting subjects for each other.

45 A week later, when the pictures were developed, so were
46 their plans for a joint project and a number of picture-taking
47 trips to various parts of the city. There were also some personal
48 developments along with the pictures and the beginning of a
49 productive partnership.

4. Phil Downs learned about photography while he was
   (A) in school
   (B) in the army
   (C) on a vacation
   (D) out of work
   (E) in the studio

5. In line 32, the word *creased* most nearly means
   (A) wrinkled
   (B) started
   (C) twitched
   (D) blinked
   (E) froze

6. The title for this story could very well be
   (A) Photography Buff
   (B) Woodland Wonders
   (C) The Darkroom
   (D) Photo Finish
   (E) A New Camera

3

Words You Need to Know

mysteriously	preventive
throbbing	agony
dispensary	miracle

---

1   Why is it every time I'm due at the dental clinic my tooth-
2   ache mysteriously disappears? Last week I had to leave work.
3   The pain and the throbbing were only part of my symptoms. I
4   was leaning over my machine at work when a sharp pain went
5   through my jaw. I guess an aspirin will fix me up, I thought. I
6   proceeded to the shop dispensary to take the tiny white pain
7   killer. The shop nurse in her crisp white uniform was as
8   unfriendly as ever.
9   "Helen," she said when I told her of my symptoms, "I really
10 think you should see a dentist right away."
11   I wrinkled my nose at this suggestion. Even as a child, I
12 used to talk my mother out of having my teeth checked. "We
13 have them cleaned at the school clinic, and that's enough for
14 me," I'd say each time she suggested that I go.
15   Mrs. Hanson continued her urging. "Taking care of your
16 teeth is really important. Actually, preventive medicine is very
17 important to good general health." The nurse was never going
18 to be satisfied until I agreed with her, so I assured her that I
19 would call the dentist as soon as I got home.
20   It was impossible to continue working. After an hour had
21 passed, the pain became so bad that I could hardly see straight.
22 I took the bus home and tried putting a hot towel on my cheek.
23 Nothing helped. That did it. I phoned the local family health
24 service, and the woman who answered seemed very concerned
25 about the tooth.
26   "There's just one problem, though," she said. "Our dentist
27 has gone for the day. He won't be able to see you until 8:30 in the
28 morning."
29   All night long the tooth throbbed. "I thought only children
30 had toothaches." The words echoed in my head. I continued to

suffer despite the aspirins and the hot towel I put over the sore area of my mouth. I worried and had little uninterrupted sleep.

Finally morning dawned, and with it dawned the fact that I was to be at the clinic in less than three hours. Miracle of miracles, the pain seemed to be gone. I felt great. Well, actually, I didn't really, but at least the steady throb of last night seemed to have disappeared. "Maybe I should cancel the appointment," I thought. "Perhaps it was just a passing pain. There's probably no need to bother the dentist, especially so early in the morning." I picked up the telephone and began to dial.

"Hey you, put down that telephone!"

"Now, where did that voice come from?"

"You heard me. I said put it down!"

The phone dropped noisily as I sat trying to identify the voice.

"Now, listen you, and listen good. Didn't you spend the whole night in agony?"

I nodded my head up and down in agreement.

"And didn't the nurse tell you that you should have gone to the dentist BEFORE you had the trouble with your teeth?"

Again I nodded my head, yes.

"Well then, there's no time like the present. You keep that appointment. And, the next time, well, maybe there won't have to be a next time."

I smiled as I started to get dressed and silently thanked myself for the good advice.

7. The main idea of the story is that
   (A) aspirin will relieve pain from a toothache
   (B) only children have toothaches
   (C) miracles are performed in dental clinics
   (D) preventive medicine is important to good health
   (E) toothaches are less painful in the morning

8. After getting a toothache, the main character in the passage
   (A) went home
   (B) took an aspirin
   (C) called the dentist
   (D) used a hot towel
   (E) saw the nurse

9. When the main character listened to the voice (lines 43-56), she was really listening to her
    (A) nurse
    (B) self
    (C) dentist
    (D) mother
    (E) best friend

4

Words You Need to Know

twang	elevator
indicated	prodded
confidence	benefit

---

1 Stanley and Ella stood by the elevator in the West New
2 York Apartment House. They both were nervous just thinking
3 about dealing with the manager. Everyone said that this
4 manager had a thing about blacks renting in the building. But
5 Stanley decided to take a chance.
6   The meeting was arranged by telephone, and the secretary
7 repeated "two o'clock sharp." The sound of the click as the
8 secretary hung up didn't add to Stanley's confidence.
9   It was only one-thirty. Ella had pushed and prodded her
10 husband through his shower and dressing to get him there on
11 time. Soon it would be decided. Would the manager rent them
12 an apartment or would he give them the same song and dance
13 that he'd given other couples just like them? The elevator
14 ground to a stop on the fifth floor. Three passengers got out and
15 only two others remained besides Ella and Stanley.
16   "I think it's a shame the way they're letting just anybody
17 rent now, don't you, Cora?" The statement came from a short,
18 gray-haired woman standing to the rear of the car.

The other woman piped up in a twangy, high-pitched voice, "I'll say. Our old manager had a little pride about who came and went around here. We'll have to have a little talk with this new manager. We'll remind him that some of our rent pays his salary."

Without a backward glance, the two women left the elevator on the seventh floor. Neither of them had enough courage to look at the black couple although the conversation had obviously been spoken for their benefit.

"Now that does it!" Stanley doubled up a fist and he pounded it into the palm of his other hand. "Those fools don't give a man a chance. I don't want to live in a place where I'm not wanted. No sir. Not me." The veins in his neck became twice their normal size as he spoke, and you could almost see his blood pressure go up.

Ella put her arm gently on Stanley's shoulder. "Baby, I know how you feel. I'd like to have hit both of them back there. But that's just no way to handle this. You know and I know that we have the right to move into this building or any other. How do those people come off thinking that we're not good enough to live in the same building with them?"

They left the elevator at the ninth floor and proceeded down the hall as the sign indicated. The office was just around the corner.

"Go right in," the secretary motioned to the inner office. "He's waiting for you."

The man behind the desk rose slowly to his feet and extended his hand. "I'm the new manager of the building, John Stevens."

Stanley blinked his eyes in surprise. Standing before them was John Stevens, and he was all of six feet tall, handsomely dressed, and . . . he was black.

Later, after the lease was signed, Stanley told the manager about the two women in the elevator.

"Oh," said Mr. Stevens, "I'm afraid you don't understand. The Simpson sisters are upset about the new city councilman from this district who just moved in across the hall from them. In their opinion, renting to politicians is like opening the door for a burglar."

10. The title for this story could very well be
    (A) The Times Are Changing
    (B) The Inner Office
    (C) Apartment Living
    (D) The Seventh Floor
    (E) Taking a Chance

11. The Simpson sisters were
    (A) concerned about the manager's salary
    (B) gossiping about Stanley and Ella
    (C) complaining about a new tenant
    (D) angry with people on the elevator
    (E) concerned about the care of the building

12. When the author says, "The veins in his neck became twice their normal size" (lines 31-32), she means Stanley
    (A) was having a heart attack
    (B) became angry
    (C) sweated heavily
    (D) showed excitement
    (E) became sick

5

Words You Need to Know

activated	vital
sensation	frantically
duplicate	responsibility

1　　Joe Webster had a job. After weeks of searching for work,
2　he'd finally had some luck. Oh, it wasn't much. Joe was doing
3　odd jobs at the local steel mill, sort of general, all-around
4　handyman you might say. "Well, it's better than sitting around
5　all day looking at the four walls," Joe had told himself and even
6　said it quietly to Lila, his wife of two years.

All Joe's luck had seemed to leave after his first wife left him. Jessie had been a good woman, but she had found someone else while Joe was in the army in Vietnam. Ever since the divorce and his own hard times after he came back from the war, things had just gone downhill for Joe.

"If only I'd had a chance to finish school," thought Joe. "When Pop died, there wasn't anyone else but me to help out."

Joe had been on his new job three weeks when it all happened. He had just finished picking up the trash buckets and sweeping out Mr. Henderson's office when a strange odor hit his nostrils. Joe looked around but couldn't really find anything unusual. It was time to lock up, and Joe paid close attention to what he was doing because it was his responsibility to check all doors and windows. The company had government contracts, and much of the information kept at the plant was top secret and vital to the military.

Joe swung the old Ford out of the mill yard and was heading toward Baker Street and his own neighborhood. But a nagging sensation tugged at him. "Oh, I might as well go back and check one more time. There's something funny about that smell I noticed. It's like the way the trash smells when I'm burning old plastic layouts from finished projects."

Joe reached the file room just in time to see the flames reaching out toward the paper lying on the shelf above the filing cabinet. He dashed out to the security section of the building and activated the sprinkler system. Something was jammed. Joe frantically worked to correct the problem. After the sprinklers began working, Joe called the local fire station. Then Joe quickly phoned Mr. Henderson, the plant manager, to alert him to what was happening. Joe ran back to the file room and grabbed an armload of the papers and plastic plans. He made four more trips until there was nothing left on the steel shelving.

Mr. Henderson arrived with the fire trucks. "Joe! Joe! Are you all right?" Mr. Henderson's voice rang out in the darkened hall.

Joe was sitting in the hall, against the wall next to a pile of papers.

"My God," his boss cried out, "look at your hands." Joe's hands had been burned and cut.

"Well, at least I got all your papers out in time, Mr. Henderson."

Mr. Henderson picked up a few of the plastic sheets. "Didn't you know that we always lock up the government plans at the end of the day? All the important papers are kept in a fireproof safe. The plans you risked your life to save are nothing more than duplicates of the plans."

Joe was miserable. He could easily have been killed in the fire, and it all would have been for nothing. It was just one more piece of bad luck. Why hadn't he just gone home?

Joe was just about to tell Mr. Henderson that he was nothing but a loser and that maybe Mr. Henderson would be better off without him. But, before he had a chance to speak, Mr. Henderson started talking again. "Joe, I don't want you to think that I don't appreciate what you did tonight. You may not have saved any vital government plans, but you did save my factory. I'm proud to have a man like you working for me. As a matter of fact, I happen to know that there is a trainee's job open in the factory. The union owes me a favor, and I think I can help you get that job if you're interested. I'll talk to the union boss in the morning. Come see me at ten o'clock, and we'll talk about it."

As Mr. Henderson disappeared down the hall to talk to the firemen, Joe smiled to himself. Maybe his luck was about to change after all.

13. Joe's decision to return to the mill was based on his
    (A) unwillingness to go home
    (B) desire to get a raise
    (C) adventurous spirit
    (D) feeling of responsibility
    (E) sick feeling

14. Before the fire broke out in the mill, Joe had been working for
    (A) three months
    (B) three weeks
    (C) thirty days
    (D) three years
    (E) sixty days

15. When the author says, "a nagging sensation tugged at him" (lines 24-25), she means
    (A) he had a backache
    (B) he was afraid to drive in his neighborhood
    (C) his passenger pulled at his jacket
    (D) he felt that something was wrong
    (E) he thought his wife would be angry

ANSWERS AND EXPLANATIONS—UNIT V

Finding Supporting Details

1. **(C)** is the only supporting detail given in the passage, as a requirement for getting a driver's license (See lines 45-47). Although the passage does state that you *can* go to a driving school or practice driving with a relative, it does not state that you *must* do so. Therefore, answers (A) and (D) are incorrect. Nowhere in the passage does it say that you must own a car or have your picture taken; therefore, answers (B) and (E) are incorrect.

Following Sequence

2. **(E)** is the first event in the sequence of events that lead up to getting a driver's license. This is stated in lines 2-3.

Finding the Main Idea

3. **(D)** is the best answer. The whole selection is about the steps a person must take in getting a driver's license.

Finding Supporting Details

4. **(B)** is the correct answer. The fact that Phil Downs learned about photography in the army is stated in line 5.

Making Inferences

5. **(A)** is the answer. The sentence goes on to state that he was grinning broadly. Usually, when one smiles, the face wrinkles.

Finding the Main Idea

6. **(D)** is the best answer. All kinds of good things happened as a result of the photography class. Paul was not a photography buff (A). The story is not about a new camera (E), the darkroom (C), or woodland wonders (B).

Finding the Main Idea

7. **(D)** is the answer. The main idea is stated in lines 16-17 and is dramatized by the fact that Helen, in lines 54-56, feels that there may not be a next time if she takes care of her teeth now.

Following Sequence	8. **(E)**	is the correct answer. It is stated in line 7.
Making Inferences	9. **(B)**	is the correct answer. You can make this inference from the fact that Helen "thanked myself for the good advice" (lines 57-58).
Finding the Main Idea	10. **(A)**	is the best answer. The fact that Mr. Stevens treated Stanley and Ella in a just and fair manner, and that he rented them an apartment in a building that had the reputation for not renting to Blacks, indicates that the times are changing—at least in this building. None of the other answer choices deal with this important aspect of the story.
Finding Supporting Details	11. **(C)**	is the correct answer. It is stated in the last paragraph.
Making Inferences	12. **(B)**	is the best answer. You can make this inference based on the angry words Stanley speaks, the fact that he pounded a fist into his palm, and the fact that "you could almost see his blood pressure go up."
Making Inferences	13. **(D)**	is the best answer. Joe went back to the mill because he thought that he recognized the strange odor as the smell of something burning. Only answer (D) gives an explanation for why he would act on this thought.
Finding Supporting Details	14. **(B)**	is the correct answer. It is stated in line 14.

Making Inferences

15. **(D)** is the best answer. When Joe first notices the strange odor, he looks around for something "unusual" (lines 16-18). It is this feeling that something unusual was going on that "nagged" at him. None of the other choices are supported by details in the selection.

UNIT V: READING SELECTIONS—
EVALUATION CHART

In order to see how well you've done on the Unit V Reading Selections, see which questions you got right and which ones you got wrong. Then check against the chart below to find out which, if any, types of questions gave you trouble.

Circle the numbers of the questions you got right in the chart below. Enter the number of right answers of each type and the total.

Reading Skill	Question Numbers	Number of Correct Answers	Study Pages
Finding the Main Idea	3, 6, 7, 10		19-26
Finding Supporting Details	1, 4, 11, 13, 14		20-23
Following Sequence	2, 8		29-34
Making Inferences	9, 12, 15		37-42
Making Inferences About Word Meaning	5		173-181

Total number of correct answers _____

UNIT VI: FOLLOWING DIRECTIONS

When you read directions, you find out how to do something. This is one of the most important purposes of reading. When you buy any mechanical appliance, from something as complicated as a stereo to something as simple as a toaster, you are given printed directions on how to operate it. You follow directions to get to a place you've never been before, to cook something from a recipe, and to fill out important forms such as job applications, deposit slips, and license applications.

The following suggestions will help you to follow directions more efficiently:

1. Read through the directions quickly to get a general idea of what you have to do.

2. Read the directions again, making sure that they make sense. (Why does step 1 go before step 2?)

3. Note guiding words such as *first, then, after, before, now,* and *finally*. These words tell you which step follows which.

4. Review the directions mentally before you use them.

Cooking from a recipe requires you to follow directions carefully, otherwise you can end up with something that goes into the garbage rather than on the table.

Exercise A

DIRECTIONS: Read the following recipe for Texas Kidney Bean-Chili Soup and answer the questions that follow it. Check your answers in the Answer Key at the end of the unit.

Texas Kidney Bean-Chili Soup

2 cups dried red kidney beans, washed and drained
6 cups water
1 large bay leaf
4 sprigs parsley
salt, pepper to taste
2 medium-sized onions, peeled and chopped
2 garlic cloves, crushed
2 tablespoons vegetable oil
1-2 teaspoons chili powder
2 pounds lean ground beef
4 cups tomato juice
2 cups chopped green pepper

Put the beans in a large kettle and add the water, bay leaf, parsley, salt and pepper. Bring to a boil; boil for 2 minutes. Remove from the stove and let stand for 1 hour. Return to the stove and simmer, covered, for 1 hour. While the beans are cooking, cook the onions and garlic in the oil in a skillet over low heat until tender. Stir in the chili powder and cook several seconds. Push the onions aside and add the beef. Cook slowly, breaking apart the meat with a fork, until the redness disappears. Remove from the stove and set aside. After the beans have cooked for 1 hour, add the onion-beef mixture and the tomato juice. Mix well and continue to simmer another 30 minutes or until the beans are tender. Add the chopped pepper 5 minutes before the cooking is finished. Season to taste and remove from the heat. Take out and discard the parsley sprigs and bay leaf. Serves 6.
Note: if the dish is prepared beforehand, add the green peppers after it is reheated.

1. How much time will it take you to cook Texas Kidney Bean-Chili Soup?

2. Cook the onions and garlic
   (A) for one hour
   (B) while the beans are cooking
   (C) over a high flame
   (D) for several seconds
   (E) until they are brown

3. What is the last ingredient to be added to this soup?

4. Which of the original ingredients are not in the finished soup?

5. How many different pots will you need to prepare this soup?

A number of games people play to relax are also based on following directions.

Exercise B

DIRECTIONS: Connect the dots according to numbers one to ten. Then compare the diagram you have drawn to the one in the Answer Key at the end of the chapter.

A.   .E

B.   .D

              C.

1. Connect A to B   2. Connect A to C
3. Connect A to D   4. Connect A to E
5. Connect B to C   6. Connect B to D
7. Connect B to E   8. Connect C to D
9. Connect C to E   10. Connect D to E

Exercise C

When you want to put money into a savings or checking account, you must fill out a deposit form to give to the bank teller along with your deposit. Although deposit forms from different banks may look a little different, almost all of them require the same information. It is important to fill out the deposit form carefully so that it is accurate when you give it to the bank teller; otherwise, your account might not be properly credited.

DIRECTIONS: Read the paragraph below, and then fill in the blanks in the sentences that follow. Check your answers in the Answer Key at the end of the unit.

On October 19, 1983, John Marshall deposited some money into his savings account No. H23458. He endorsed (signed on the back) three checks for deposit and wanted $76 cash returned to him. Because his mind was on other things, he ended up having to fill out three deposit forms before he was finished. The checks were for $138.20, $55, and $23.45. Which of the deposit slips shown opposite should John have given to the teller? What errors can you find on the other two forms?

John should give deposit slip ____ to the teller.

Errors on deposit slip 1 _____

Errors on deposit slip 2 _____

Errors on deposit slip 3 _____

FOLLOWING DIRECTIONS 81

Savings Account	**Savings Account**	**Savings Account**
DEPOSIT FORM TO FEDERAL SAVINGS	**DEPOSIT FORM** TO FEDERAL SAVINGS	**DEPOSIT FORM** TO FEDERAL SAVINGS
Savings Account No. H23453	Savings Account No. H23458	Savings Account No. H23458
Name John Marshall	Name John Marshall	Name John Marshall
Date October 19, 19__	Date October 19, 19 83	Date October 19, 19 83
	DOLLARS | CENTS	DOLLARS | CENTS	DOLLARS | CENTS
CASH			138 | 20
CHECKS (Please list amount of each check separately)	138 | 20 55 | 00 23 | 45 PLEASE ENDORSE ALL CHECKS	138 | 20 55 | 00 23 | 45 PLEASE ENDORSE ALL CHECKS	78 | 45 PLEASE ENDORSE ALL CHECKS
TOTAL CASH & CHECKS	216 | 65	216 | 65	216 | 65
DEPOSIT		140 | 65	140 | 65
AMOUNT RETURNED	76 | 00	76 | 00	76 | 00

deposit slip **1**   deposit slip **2**   deposit slip **3**

82 FOLLOWING DIRECTIONS

Exercise D

Laura Ann Murray was born on June 12, 1960, the only daughter of Samuel E. and Mary Sue Murray, in Queens County, New York City. Before her marriage to Sam, Mary Sue's name was Mary Sue Stewart. Laura lives with her family at 97-20 57th Avenue, Rego Park, New York 11368. On September 13, 1976, Laura went to the Social Security Administration Office to apply for a Social Security number. Laura was hoping to get a part-time job at the record store near school, but she knew that she would have to apply for a social security number since she had never gotten one before. The only other job that she had held was as a volunteer worker for her father's political organization, the German-American Club. At the Social Security Administration Office, she was handed a form like the one you see below.

DIRECTIONS: Following the instructions on the form, and using the information you know about Laura, fill it out for her. Then carefully compare your form to the one in the Answer Key at the end of the chapter.

```
ID              CN              DO
APPLICATION FOR A SOCIAL SECURITY NUMBER         DO NOT WRITE IN THE ABOVE SPACE
See Instructions on Back.   Print in Black or Dark Blue Ink or Use Typewriter.

1  Print FULL NAME        (First Name)    (Middle Name or Initial – if none, draw line ___)    (Last Name)
   YOU WILL USE IN WORK
   OR BUSINESS

2  Print FULL                                                          6  YOUR    (Month) (Day) (Year)
   NAME GIVEN                                                             DATE OF
   YOU AT BIRTH                                                           BIRTH

3  PLACE       (City)          (County if known)        (State)         7  YOUR PRESENT AGE
   OF                                                                     (Age on last birthday)
   BIRTH

4  MOTHER'S FULL NAME AT HER BIRTH (Her maiden name)                    8  YOUR SEX
                                                                           MALE   FEMALE

5  FATHER'S FULL NAME (Regardless of whether living or dead)            9  YOUR COLOR OR RACE
                                                                           WHITE  NEGRO  OTHER

10 HAVE YOU EVER BEFORE APPLIED FOR    DON'T  (If "YES" Print STATE in which you applied and DATE you applied and SOCIAL SECURITY NUMBER if known)
   OR HAD A UNITED STATES SOCIAL   NO  KNOW YES
   SECURITY, RAILROAD, OR TAX ACCOUNT
   NUMBER?

11 YOUR        (Number and Street, Apt. No., P.O. Box, or Rural Route)   (City)        (State)      (Zip Code)
   MAILING
   ADDRESS

12 TODAY'S DATE          NOTICE: Whoever, with intent to falsify his or someone else's true identity, willfully furnishes or causes to be
                         furnished false information in applying for a social security number, is subject to a fine of not more than $1,000
                         or imprisonment for up to 1 year, or both.

13 TELEPHONE NUMBER   14 Sign YOUR NAME HERE (Do Not Print)

FORM SS-5 (5-74)           [ ]RESCREEN   [ ]ASSIGN   [ ]DUP ISSUED   Return completed application to nearest
                                                                     SOCIAL SECURITY ADMINISTRATION OFFICE
```

ANSWER KEY—UNIT VI

Exercise A

1. 2 hours and 32 minutes

    It takes 2 minutes to boil the beans, bay leaf, parsley, salt, and pepper; 1 hour to let the beans stand; 1 hour to simmer the beans while the other ingredients are cooking; and 30 minutes to cook everything together.

2. (B)

    Answers (C) and (E) are incorrect according to the recipe. There is no support for answers (A) and (D). The recipe says that the onions and garlic are cooked until tender. Then they are cooked with chili powder for several seconds. And then they are cooked with the beef until the redness disappears. It is impossible to tell, from the recipe, exactly how much time these steps will take.

3. chopped pepper

4. parsley sprigs and bay leaf

5. 2—a kettle and a skillet

Exercise B

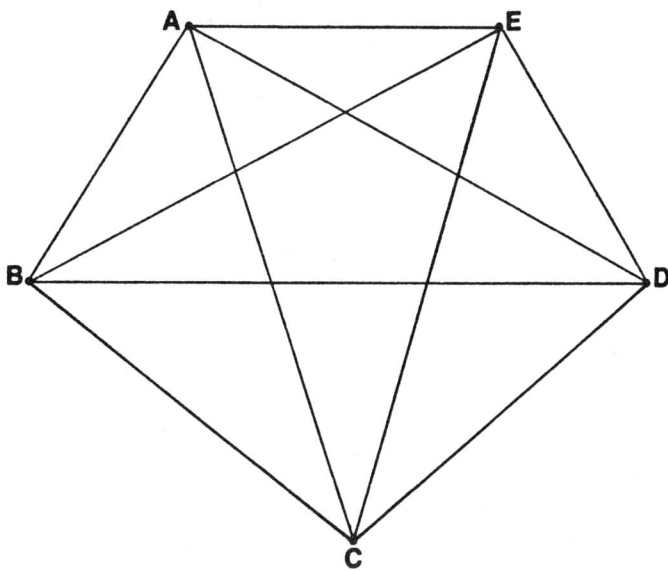

84 FOLLOWING DIRECTIONS

Exercise C

1. John should give deposit slip 2 to the teller.

2. Errors on deposit slip 1:   The account number is incorrect.
   The year is not filled in.
   The deposit amount is not filled in.

   Errors on deposit slip 3:   One check is listed in the section of the form marked CASH.
   The other two checks are not listed separately, as the instructions say that they should be.

Exercise D

ID	CN	DO	DO NOT WRITE IN THE ABOVE SPACE

APPLICATION FOR A SOCIAL SECURITY NUMBER
See Instructions on Back.   Print in Black or Dark Blue Ink or Use Typewriter.

1. Print FULL NAME YOU WILL USE IN WORK OR BUSINESS — (First Name) Laura   (Middle Name or Initial — if none, draw line ___) Ann   (Last Name) Murray

2. Print FULL NAME GIVEN YOU AT BIRTH — Laura Ann Murray

6. YOUR DATE OF BIRTH (Month) (Day) (Year): 6 / 12 / 60

3. PLACE OF BIRTH — (City) New York City   (County if known) Queens   (State) New York

7. YOUR PRESENT AGE (Age on last birthday): 16

4. MOTHER'S FULL NAME AT HER BIRTH (Her maiden name) — Mary Sue Stewart

8. YOUR SEX — MALE ☐ FEMALE ☒

5. FATHER'S FULL NAME (Regardless of whether living or dead) — Samuel E. Murray

9. YOUR COLOR OR RACE — WHITE ☒ NEGRO ☐ OTHER ☐

10. HAVE YOU EVER BEFORE APPLIED FOR OR HAD A UNITED STATES SOCIAL SECURITY, RAILROAD, OR TAX ACCOUNT NUMBER? — NO ☒ DON'T KNOW ☐ YES ☐   (If "YES" Print STATE in which you applied and DATE you applied and SOCIAL SECURITY NUMBER if known)

11. YOUR MAILING ADDRESS — (Number and Street, Apt. No., P.O. Box, or Rural Route) 97-20 57th Avenue   (City) Rego Park,   (State) New York   (Zip Code) 11368

12. TODAY'S DATE — 9/13/76

14. NOTICE: Whoever, with intent to falsify his or someone else's true identity, willfully furnishes or causes to be furnished false information in applying for a social security number, is subject to a fine of not more than $1,000 or imprisonment for up to 1 year, or both.

13. TELEPHONE NUMBER

Sign YOUR NAME HERE (Do Not Print) — *Laura Ann Murray*

FORM SS-5 (5-74)   ☐ RESCREEN   ☐ ASSIGN   ☐ DUP ISSUED   Return completed application to nearest SOCIAL SECURITY ADMINISTRATION OFFICE

UNIT VII: SEEING RELATIONSHIPS

Study the pictures below. What is the same in each picture? What is different? Fill in your answers in the blanks below each picture.

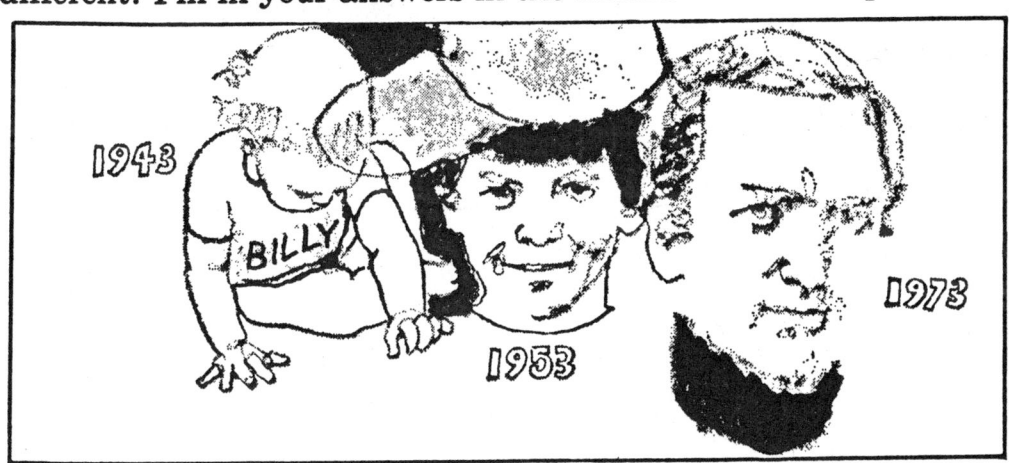

1. Similarities: _____

   Differences: _____

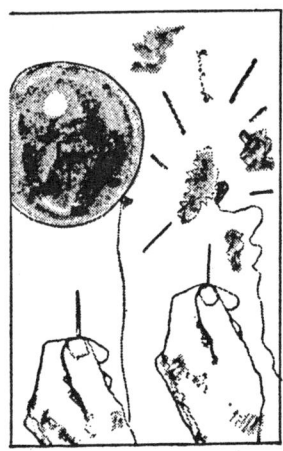

2. Similarities: _____

   Differences: _____

86   SEEING RELATIONSHIPS

3. Similarities: _____

   Differences: _____

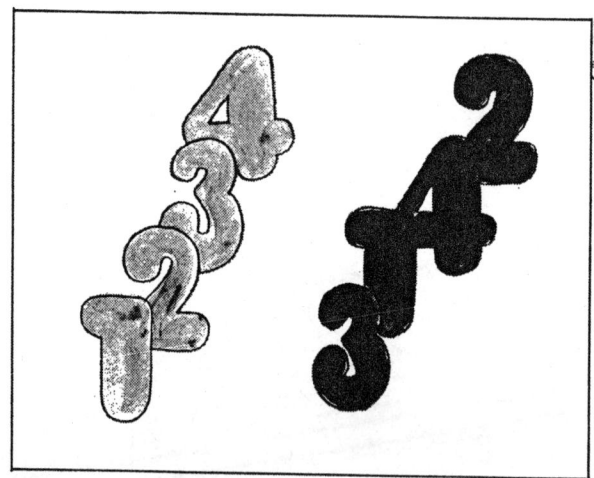

4. Similarities: _____

   Differences: _____

SEEING RELATIONSHIPS 87

5. Similarities: _____

   Differences: _____

   As you read, you will often notice similarities and differences between things just as you have done with the pictures on the preceding pages. When you notice similarities and differences, you are finding a relationship between the two things. Looking back at the pictures, you can describe the relationships you found as being one of the following five types:

   (1) **time**—for picture number 1
   (2) **cause-effect**—for picture number 2
   (3) **compare-contrast**—for picture number 3
   (4) **order**—for picture number 4
   (5) **part-whole**—for picture number 5

   In your reading, you will find these same five types of relationships. Knowing how these types of relationships work will help you organize the information you read. On the following pages, you will find five different paragraphs. As you read, try to find out what type of relationship the writer is using. If you understand the relationship, you will be able to answer the questions that follow the paragraphs.

SEEING RELATIONSHIPS

The train rolled along the steel rails. In five minutes it was due to arrive at Wayman's Crossing. Just outside Wayman's Crossing, a young boy had gotten his foot caught in the tracks. Help was just ten minutes away. A friend was leading the boy's father to the track at that moment. The train had to stop at Wayman's Crossing to take on water—that would only take four minutes. Once the train started up again, it would cross the spot where the boy stood in less than two minutes.

Will help arrive in time? _____

In order to answer the question, you must understand the **time relationship** involved. First, you must find out how much time it will take for the train to arrive at the spot where the boy is trapped. It will take five minutes for the train to reach Wayman's Crossing, plus four minutes to stop to take on water, plus less than two minutes to travel from Wayman's Crossing to the boy; that is a total of just less than eleven minutes (5 + 4 + 2 = 11). Once you know this, you must find out how much time it will take for help to arrive. Looking back at the paragraph, you find the sentence: *Help was just ten minutes away.* That is one minute less than it will take for the train to reach the same spot. Therefore, the answer to the question is: Yes, help will arrive in time.

Now read the next paragraph.

Before the Civil War, all of the United States' warships were built of wood. Then, in 1862, the Confederates covered the wooden warship *Merrimack* with iron plates. Spies from the North learned of the Confederate ship. Frightened by the possibilities, the North built an iron ship named the *Monitor*. On March 8, 1862, the *Merrimack* sailed from Norfolk, Virginia, to attack the wooden warships *Cumberland* and *Congress,* which were stationed just up the James River at Newport News. The iron ship easily sank both of the wooden ships. To protect their position on the James River, the Union brought in their own iron ship, the *Monitor*. On March 9, the two iron ships began the battle that would change history. Although neither ship came out of the battle with a clear victory, the two ships did prove the value of having iron ships.

Why did the North have to bring in the *Monitor* to protect their position on the James River? _____

SEEING RELATIONSHIPS   89

To answer this question, you must understand the **cause-effect relationship** involved. The question tells you that something happened and asks you to find the cause. Looking back at the paragraph, you will find the statement that the Confederate ship *Merrimack* easily sank two wooden ships. Since wooden ships could not defeat the *Merrimack*, the Union sailors could only hope to protect themselves by bringing in their own iron ship, the *Monitor*. Your answer should explain that fact.

You can find another cause-effect relationship in this paragraph. You are told that the two iron ships began a battle (cause) that would change history (effect). You may have to do a little thinking to understand why this was the cause that produced this particular effect. You will have to go back to the first sentence to read that *"Before the Civil War, all of the United States' warships were built of wood."* You must then assume that the battle between the two iron ships—a battle that *"proved the value of iron ships"*—marked the end of the age of the wooden warship.

Now read the next paragraph.

Julio Lopez decided that he would have to buy a car to get to his new job since there were no buses that would get him there. He went down to the used car lot, but he couldn't make up his mind. He narrowed it down to choosing between two cars—a small economy car and a station wagon. He liked the lower price of the economy car, and he liked the idea of getting 24 miles for every gallon of gas. However, he would be able to carry building supplies and tools in the station wagon. The station wagon only got 17 miles for every gallon of gas, but it was bigger and could be used for many things besides going to work.

If Julio only uses the car to travel back and forth to work, which car should he buy? _____

To answer this question, you must set up a **compare-contrast relationship.** You must compare the two cars to find out which one is best for Julio's purposes. You can do this by setting up a chart:

economy car	*station wagon*
less expensive	more expensive
24 miles per gallon	17 miles per gallon
small	large

SEEING RELATIONSHIPS

By comparing the qualities of one car to the qualities of the other, you can decide that the economy car is the best one for Julio. He will get better gas mileage and will spend less money. Since he only needs the car to drive himself back and forth to work, he doesn't need the larger car.

Now, read the next paragraph.

Dick just started a new job as an auto mechanic for Ace Auto Repair. On his first day, the boss told him that he could find any part he wanted on the shelves and bins in the parts room. In the parts room, everything is arranged in alphabetical order. For example, carburetors are on the shelves next to the bins containing ball bearings.

If Dick is standing in front of a shelf labeled mufflers, will he find brake parts stored before or after the spot where he is standing? _____

To answer this question, you must understand the **relationship of order** between the parts in the parts room. Looking back at the paragraph, you find the statement that *"everything is arranged in alphabetical order."* Since *b* comes before *m* in the alphabet, *b*rake parts will be shelved before *m*ufflers.

Now, read the last paragraph.

McCabe was the newly elected president of the club. He was not sure of himself as the meeting began. Arguments started, and each side began shouting. McCabe watched. Soon, the room became so noisy that no one could be heard. McCabe pounded on the table and shouted, "Will everyone be quiet for a moment? Let's give each person a chance to speak. Mr. Garcia, let's start with you."

Why was McCabe able to bring the meeting to order? _____

To answer this question, you must understand the relationship between McCabe and the group as a whole (a **part-whole relationship**). Looking back at the first sentence, you read that McCabe is the president of the club. One duty of a president is to keep order at club meetings. Thus, the answer to the question is: because McCabe is the president of the club.

To test your ability to find relationships, do the following exercise. By understanding the relationship between the first two things, you will be able to choose the answer that will set up the same relationship between the third and fourth.

Exercise A

DIRECTIONS: In each of the following sentences, there is a relationship between the first two things. Choose the answer choice that will have the same relationship to the third thing in the sentence. Circle your answer. Correct answers are given in the Answer Key at the end of the unit. The first one is done for you as an example.

1. One is to three as A is to
    (A) B
    (B) D
    (C) Z
    (D) C

2. Finger is to hand as toe is to
    (A) head
    (B) foot
    (C) shoe
    (D) walk

3. Red is to pink as black is to
    (A) gray
    (B) white
    (C) green
    (D) yellow

4. Burn is to blister as bump is to
    (A) fracture
    (B) bruise
    (C) pain
    (D) clumsy

5. Sunday is to Monday as Wednesday is to
   (A) Tuesday
   (B) Thursday
   (C) Friday
   (D) Saturday

6. Cook is to eat as crawl is to
   (A) walk
   (B) sit
   (C) turn
   (D) lie

7. Engine is to car as heart is to
   (A) center
   (B) blood
   (C) soul
   (D) body

8. Car is to truck as cat is to
   (A) dog
   (B) lion
   (C) kitten
   (D) deer

9. Heat is to melt as cold is to
   (A) winter
   (B) thaw
   (C) freeze
   (D) refrigerator

10. Sunrise is to sunset as breakfast is to
    (A) lunch
    (B) eggs
    (C) brunch
    (D) dinner

SEEING RELATIONSHIPS

Understanding relationships will help you get information out of a story even when the writer does not give you that information directly. In the following exercise, for example, you will read a short paragraph about a family. Even though the writer does not tell you the answers to the questions that follow the paragraph, you will be able to get the answers by understanding the relationships that are explained in the story.

Exercise B

DIRECTIONS: Read the paragraph below and then answer the questions that follow the paragraph. Fill in your answers in the blanks provided. Answers are given in the Answer Key at the end of the unit.

When Aunt Gale married Uncle Don in September of 1935, she moved into many new relationships. She was eighteen that September and Don was four years older. He came from a large family, and most of his relatives lived in California. The only people Gale met at the wedding were Don's twin brother Steve and his wife Elaine, my parents. I wasn't born until a year later. I guess it was because my father and Don were twins that he became my favorite uncle.

1. In what year was Gale born? _____
2. In what year was Don born? _____
3. How old was Steve when the writer was born? _____
4. What is the relationship between Gale and Elaine? _____
5. Which came first: (a) the writer's birth or (b) Gale's wedding?

94 SEEING RELATIONSHIPS

ANSWER KEY—UNIT VII

Picture Exercise on pages 85-87

1. Similarities: All three illustrations show males.

   Differences: Each illustration shows the male at a different **time.**

2. Similarities: Both illustrations show a hand holding a pin or needle.
   Both show balloons.

   Differences: In the first illustration, the balloon is whole. In the second illustration, the pin has **caused** the balloon to burst.

3. Similarities. Both illustrations show watches.

   Differences: The first watch is definitely for a woman; the second could be for anyone. The first watch tells only the time. The second watch tells the date as well as the time.

4. Similarities: Both illustrations show the same four numbers.

   Differences: The two sets of numbers are not written in the same **order.**

5. Similarities: Both illustrations show an orange.

   Differences: The first illustration shows a **whole** orange; the second only **parts** of an orange.

Exercise A

1. (D) C

   This is a relationship of order. Just as the number 3 is two steps higher than 1, the letter C is two letters up the alphabet from A.

2. (B) foot

   This is a part-whole relationship. Just as a finger is a part of the hand, a toe is a part of the foot.

SEEING RELATIONSHIPS   95

3. (A) gray

    This is a compare-contrast relationship. Just as pink is a light shade of red, gray is a light shade of black.

4. (B) bruise

    This is a cause-effect relationship. Just as a burn is the cause of a blister, a bump is the cause of a bruise.

5. (B) Thursday

    This is a time relationship. Just as Sunday is the day before Monday, Wednesday is the day before Thursday.

6. (A) walk

    This is a relationship of order. Just as you must cook something before you eat it, you must learn to crawl before you can walk.

7. (D) body

    This is a part-whole relationship. Just as the engine is a part of a car, the heart is a part of the body.

8. (B) lion

    This is a compare-contrast relationship. Just as a car is a smaller means of transportation than a truck, a cat is a smaller member of the cat family than a lion.

9. (C) freeze

    This is a cause-effect relationship. Just as heat causes something to melt, cold causes something to freeze.

10. (D) dinner

    This is a time relationship. Just as sunrise comes before sunset, breakfast is eaten before dinner.

Exercise B

1. Gale was born in 1917.

    You will have to understand the time relationship involved to answer this question. If Gale was 18 when she got married in 1935, she was born 18 years before that year: 1935 − 18 = 1917.

2. Don was born in 1913.

    Again, you will have to understand a time relationship. If Don was four years older than Gale, he was born four years before she was: 1917 - 4 = 1913.

3. Steve was 23 years old when the writer was born.

    First, you must notice that Don and Steve are twin brothers, which makes them the same age (this is a compare-contrast relationship). Once you know that you must figure out Don's age. If Don was four years older than Gale in 1935, and if Gale was 18 in 1935, that would make Don 22 years old when he was married in 1935. The writer also tells you that she/he was not born until a year later, which would make Don 23 years old at that time. Since Don and Steve are the same age, Steve was 23 years old when the writer was born.

4. Gale and Elaine are sisters-in-law.

    This is a cause-effect relationship. Gale and Elaine married brothers (cause), which makes them sisters-in-law (effect).

5. (b) Gale's wedding came first.

    This is another time relationship. The writer states that she/he was not born until the year after Gale and Don's wedding.

UNIT VIII: VOCABULARY SKILLS—
DIVIDING WORDS INTO SYLLABLES

Read these three words:

      to   get   her

Now combine them to form one word:

      together

Notice that, even though the letters are the same, *to get her* is not pronounced the same way as *together*. This is because the **units of sound** or **syllables** that make up the word *together* are:

      to   geth   er

Breaking up words into units of sound is called **syllabication.**

The sounds in written words are represented by syllables. Each syllable represents one unit of sound. Learning how to divide a word into syllables is useful for two reasons. First, if you are trying to spell a word, the best way to do it is to sound it out syllable by syllable. Second, if you're reading a word for the first time, the best way to figure out how to pronounce it is by dividing it into syllables.

Every syllable contains a letter called a vowel. The vowels are *a, e, i, o, u,* and *y* when it has the sound of *e* or *i* as in *city* or *sky*. The other letters in our alphabet are called consonants. Generally, there is at least one consonant in a syllable, although it is possible to have a syllable that consists of only a vowel. In studying syllabication, you will notice that sometimes two vowels combine to form one vowel sound. These vowels should not be split up when you are dividing a word into syllables. Remember, syllables are units of sound.

The following exercises will teach you some of the rules of syllabication.

98 VOCABULARY SKILLS—DIVIDING WORDS INTO SYLLABLES

Exercise A

DIRECTIONS: Look at the words in the following chart and fill in the three boxes next to each. The first one is done for you as an example. Check your answers in the Answer Key at the end of the unit.

Word	Number of Vowels Seen	Number of Vowels Heard	Number of Syllables
strong	1	1	1
preheat			
love			
complaint			
coffee			
fearful			
boating			
steam			
careless			
meat			
cheese			

VOCABULARY SKILLS—DIVIDING WORDS INTO SYLLABLES

Words are split between two consonants to show syllables.

Exercise B

DIRECTIONS: Divide the following words into syllables using *hyphens* (-). Check your answers in the Answer Key at the end of the unit.

error _____   differ _____

summer _____   pepper _____

channel _____ coffee _____

lesson _____   napkin _____

blossom _____   number _____

traffic _____   candy _____

When a syllable ends in the letters *le,* start at the *le,* move one letter to the left, and set off those three letters as a syllable. For example, you would break the word *tremble* into syllables as *trem - ble.*

Exercise C

DIRECTIONS: Divide the following words into syllables.

crumble _____   waffle _____

middle _____   fumble _____

scramble _____ giggle _____

little _____   whittle _____

thimble _____   vehicle _____

100 VOCABULARY SKILLS—DIVIDING WORDS INTO SYLLABLES

When two consonants together make one sound, for example, *ch* or *ph,* it is called a **consonant blend**. Consonant blends are always kept together when you divide a word into syllables.

Exercise D

DIRECTIONS: All of the following words contain consonant blends. Divide them into syllables.

wishful	_____	teacher	_____
thicket	_____	sketching	_____
splashing	_____	pocket	_____
racket	_____	bracket	_____
chicken	_____	fudge	_____
selfishness	_____	stocking	_____

Words have both long and short vowel sounds. A **long vowel** "says its name," as in the following words: b<u>a</u> - con; <u>a</u> - pron; p<u>ay</u> - check. When a vowel has a sound other than its name, it's called **a short vowel**. The following words all contain short vowels: <u>a</u>p - ple; str<u>a</u>p; <u>a</u>f - ter.

A long vowel ends a syllable in a word with a vowel-consonant-vowel pattern. For example: ba - con.

A short vowel does not end a syllable in a word with a vowel-consonant-vowel pattern. For example: tim - id.

Exercise E

DIRECTIONS: All of the following words contain long vowel sounds. Divide the words into syllables.

VOCABULARY SKILLS—DIVIDING WORDS INTO SYLLABLES

rival _____   tiger _____

regret _____   tuna _____

final _____   frozen _____

open _____   omit _____

silent _____   climate _____

grocer _____   total _____

DIRECTIONS: All of the following words contain short vowel sounds. Divide these words into syllables.

habit _____   salad _____

confess _____   dozen _____

forbid _____   denim _____

travel _____   melon _____

upset _____   wisdom _____

lemon _____   mercy _____

Syllabication Review

DIRECTIONS: This review combines all of the syllabication rules that you have practiced in this chapter. Use hyphens to divide each word into syllables.

meeting _____   fumble _____

able _____   wealthy _____

rifle _____   motion _____

weakness _____   revise _____

VOCABULARY SKILLS—DIVIDING WORDS INTO SYLLABLES

appear　_____　　blockade　_____

pickle　_____　　deny　_____

paper　_____　　painful　_____

pavement　_____　　occur　_____

believe　_____　　perhaps　_____

raffle　_____　　knowledge　_____

music　_____　　forest　_____

taught　_____　　under　_____

kitchen　_____　　prefer　_____

mistake　_____　　disappoint　_____

enter　_____　　stretching　_____

reckless　_____　　stolen　_____

repeat　_____　　revoke　_____

laundry　_____　　despair　_____

ANSWER KEY—UNIT VIII

Exercise A

Word	Number of Vowels Seen	Number of Vowels Heard	Number of Syllables
strong	1	1	1
preheat	3	2	2
love	2	1	1
complaint	3	2	2
coffee	3	2	2
fearful	3	2	2
boating	3	2	2
steam	2	1	1
careless	3	2	2
meat	2	1	1
cheese	3	1	1

Exercise B

er - ror   dif - fer
sum - mer   pep - per
chan - nel   cof - fee
les - son   nap - kin
blos - som   num - ber
traf - fic   can - dy

Exercise C

crum - ble
mid - dle
scram - ble
lit - tle
thim - ble

waf - fle
fum - ble
gig - gle
whit - tle
ve - hi - cle

Exercise D

wish - ful
thick - et
splash - ing
rack - et
chick - en
sel - fish - ness

teach - er
sketch - ing
pock - et
brack - et
fudge
stock - ing

Exercise E

ri - val
re - gret
fi - nal
o - pen
si - lent
gro - cer

ti - ger
tu - na
fro - zen
o - mit
cli - mate
to - tal

hab - it
con - fess
for - bid
trav - el
up - set
lem - on

sal - ad
doz - en
den - im
mel - on
wis - dom
mer - cy

VOCABULARY SKILLS—DIVIDING WORDS INTO SYLLABLES

Syllabication Review

meet - ing
a - ble
ri - fle
weak - ness
ap - pear
pick - le
pa - per
pave - ment
be - lieve
raf - fle
mu - sic
taught
kitch - en
mis - take
en - ter
reck - less
re - peat
laun - dry

fum - ble
wealth - y
mo - tion
re - vise
block - ade
de - ny
pain - ful
oc - cur
per - haps
know - ledge
for - est
un - der
pre - fer
dis - ap - point
stretch - ing
sto - len
re - voke
des - pair

UNIT IX: READING SELECTIONS

DIRECTIONS: Read the following five selections. After each selection, there are a few questions. The questions will give you a chance to review the skills you have practiced in Units I through VII. Answer each question based on the information in the selection by circling the letter of the **best** answer.

The definitions of the **Words You Need to Know**, which are listed before every selection, can be found in the **Dictionary** at the back of the book.

1

Words You Need to Know

imagine   ambition
struggle   severely
depression   prescribed

---

1 Imagine a block of cement resting on your body from your
2 neck to your knees. You cannot stand up. You are unable to
3 change your position. You must struggle to be free. Depression,
4 a very strong kind of sadness, is like having a block of cement
5 on your body. It is a force that comes from within a person. This
6 force weighs a person down.
7 When a person becomes depressed, there are many things
8 that could be the cause. Suppose someone you love dies. You feel
9 saddened by the loss. For some people, this sadness can be the
10 beginning of depression. When a person loses a job that he
11 really wants to keep, that, too, can be the beginning of depres-
12 sion. Have you ever had the feeling of being completely alone in
13 the world, alone and unloved? Try to picture what it would be
14 like to be alone on a holiday, for example, on New Year's Eve or
15 on your birthday. Many people are alone at a time when most
16 people get together for celebrating. Often, this loneliness is the
17 cause of a person's sinking into depression.

Almost everyone becomes depressed at one time or another. Almost everyone has had one of the experiences that were listed above. But, just as there are many causes of depression, there are many forms of depression that a person can have. One form of depression is the feeling of being tired all the time. A person who feels that way may want to sleep a lot. Sleep is one way in which that person can hide or escape from the sadness and unhappiness he feels. As the depression gets worse, the person loses all energy and ambition. He begins to feel that nothing he does is of any use. In the deepest forms of depression, a person may not be able to tell where he is or even what day it is. He may stop eating. He may even stop talking. A severely depressed person may just sit in a corner and not move at all.

Depression is not always serious. Some people only need a little time before they can pull themselves out of their depression. For these people, once they can get out among others again and can talk about their problem, they can find a way to cope with their problem. Sometimes, however, a person can become depressed even when he or she is with others. A large group of people at a party, all talking and laughing and having a good time, may actually make that person more depressed.

Curing depression can be more than a matter of giving a person time. At times, there is a medical reason for feeling depressed. On occasion, a person can have an uneven or unbalanced amount of certain chemicals in the body. If such a condition is found by a doctor, there is medication that can be prescribed. It is a good idea to tell a doctor if you feel depressed for a long time. Sometimes medication will help, and sometimes just having someone to talk to will lift that block of cement from your body.

1. According to the passage, a person who loses a loved one through death might
   (A) commit suicide
   (B) go shopping
   (C) visit friends
   (D) become depressed
   (E) see a doctor

2. In Paragraph 5 (lines 40-48), the writer states that depression might be caused by
   (A) going to too many parties
   (B) being alone on a special holiday
   (C) the birth of a baby
   (D) too much sleep
   (E) a medical problem

3. The main idea of the passage is that
   (A) depression is caused by many things
   (B) women get depressed more often than men
   (C) too much sleep is a cause of depression
   (D) depression usually occurs with illness
   (E) people without jobs are usually depressed

4. In Paragraph 1 (lines 1-6), a block of cement is compared to
   (A) a heavy force
   (B) the foundation of a building
   (C) a death in the family
   (D) low spirits
   (E) being alone

5. Find the line that explains how a party might affect a depressed person. Write the line below.

   _____

   _____

2

Words You Need to Know

dough   echoing
ordinary   delicious
shrinkage

1   Rose and Abe had been married for a month now. Since
2 Abe always complained about her cooking, Rose had been
3 taking cooking lessons at the local trade school. Tonight she
4 was making her first important dinner since the wedding. All
5 afternoon she worked in the kitchen, remembering all the help-
6 ful hints she'd learned in class. "Never salt the meat before it is
7 half cooked, or you will have shrinkage. Stir the flour into
8 warm water until it is smooth, then add the meat juices. Other-
9 wise the gravy will be lumpy." She could hear the teacher's
10 voice echoing across the room with all the secrets that turn an
11 ordinary cook into a successful chef.
12   The roast was cooking, the potatoes were already half
13 done, and her green bean casserole was bubbling in the oven.
14 Rose punched down the rising dough for the last time and care-
15 fully shaped the curved dinner rolls with her fingers. She
16 hummed as she worked.
17   "Abe will change his mind about my cooking after tonight.
18 He probably thinks the course has been a waste of time, but
19 he'll see." She smiled and went about setting the table. All that
20 was left to do was make the salad and shake up the ingredients
21 for the special dressing. "I'm so excited," she thought. "I can't
22 wait until Abe comes home from the shop."
23   Rose showered and tried to look as though she had been
24 relaxing all day. The door swung open and she greeted her hus-
25 band with a kiss. He returned her welcome with a giant bear
26 hug and threw his coat onto a chair in the hall.
27   Dinner was served. First came the crisp salad with its spe-
28 cial dressing. Roast beef, baked potatoes, green bean casserole,
29 and canned carrots followed. The hot rolls were baked and sat
30 steaming in a bowl in the center of the table. The butter ran

down in pools at the sides of each roll. Abe ate the salad, the roast beef, the potatoes, and three hot rolls. He made a pig out of himself with the green bean casserole and took two helpings of carrots.

When Abe finished eating, he leaned back in his chair and reached for the newspaper that was lying on the table. Rose could hardly stand it. He hadn't uttered a word during the meal.

When she could take his silence no longer, Rose almost shouted the words, "Well, how did you like it? How was the dinner? Tell me, Abe, was everything all right?"

True to his usual sense of humor, Abe replied, "The carrots were delicious."

6. When Abe said that the carrots were delicious, Rose probably felt
   (A) proud
   (B) nervous
   (C) angry
   (D) frustrated
   (E) tired

7. Rose "tried to look as though she had been relaxing all day" (lines 23-24) because
   (A) she was embarrassed about how long it took her to prepare the meal
   (B) she wanted to look good for her husband
   (C) she didn't want Abe to be concerned about how tired she was
   (D) she wanted to fool Abe into thinking that nothing was different about that night
   (E) she knew Abe didn't like her to work hard

8. The word *uttered* (line 37) most nearly means
   (A) whispered
   (B) listened to
   (C) shouted
   (D) believed
   (E) spoken

112 READING SELECTIONS

9. By becoming a good cook, Rose
   (A) made her husband unhappy
   (B) gained a lot of weight
   (C) gained personal satisfaction
   (D) no longer had to attend trade school
   (E) received more affection

10. The very first thing Abe did when he came home from the shop was
    (A) throw his coat on a chair
    (B) eat his crisp salad
    (C) give Rose a hug
    (D) take a shower
    (E) eat three hot rolls

3

Words You Need to Know

cushion   pelvis
hypnotize   century
sensations   surgery

1   When a woman learns that she is pregnant, she should go
2   to a doctor or health clinic. The care she gives her unborn child,
3   called prenatal care, is very important. The best way to learn
4   about proper prenatal care is from a doctor. A doctor can tell her
5   about what foods to eat, how much rest to get, and what kinds
6   of exercise she can do. A woman who is going to have a child
7   can also attend special classes, which are given by many
8   clinics. The father of the unborn child can also attend the
9   classes to learn how to help the woman in the months ahead.
10   In these classes, women learn about the ways in which
11   they can have the baby. One is called natural childbirth. It is
12   called natural because the woman is not given any drugs
13   during childbirth. She remains aware of every feeling. With
14   this method, the woman can even have her child at home. In
15   case she needs help, however, a trained nurse or doctor should

be present. Some of these mothers learn a way to hypnotize themselves. This is called self-hypnosis, and it helps to relax the mother before she actually gives birth to her child. Some women choose natural childbirth because they want to feel the baby being born. Other women choose this way so that the baby does not have any contact with the drugs used in hospital deliveries.

Many women are afraid of the pain they think they will feel in natural childbirth. These women choose to be given medication when they have their babies. This goes along with a normal delivery in a hospital. These mothers do not feel the sensations or movements of childbirth as clearly. There is not really any danger to either the mother or the child as long as a good doctor is present.

Sometimes there is no choice about how the baby will arrive. For example, if the pelvic area is too narrow, the doctor will be forced to perform an operation. This operation is called a Caesarian section. It got its name from a ruler of the Roman people who lived many centuries ago. Julius Caesar was the first known person to be born by surgery.

Each month the doctor measures the area of the stomach between the hip bones. This tells the doctor the size of the pelvis. A woman who has normal measurements can give birth to a baby who is large or weighs a lot. However, if the infant is larger than average, the pelvic area may not be wide enough. If this is the case, the mother may need a Caesarian section.

When a woman is going to have a Caesarian section, the doctor plans the operation for some time before the baby is due to arrive. Sometimes the date will be set two weeks ahead of the natural delivery time. The date is figured according to many factors. For example, each fetus, or baby, is wrapped inside a sac that contains liquid. This sac acts as a cushion to prevent the baby from being hurt as it moves around inside the mother. If the sac breaks earlier than expected, the mother may experience labor pains. Once labor pains occur, the Caesarian section must be performed immediately.

Since babies grow each day, doctors like to have the baby remain inside the mother for as long as possible. As the time of delivery draws near, it gets bigger and is usually in a healthier and stronger state for birth. The mother's doctor will constantly look for anything that could go wrong during childbirth. If a woman does not see her doctor regularly, she may not be aware that anything is wrong until it is too late to do anything about it.

60 Usually, a doctor will help the mother with the kind of birth
61 she would like, unless this is not possible for some medical
62 reason. Certain hospitals invite the father to watch the birth
63 process through a window or in the delivery room. There are
64 also hospitals where fathers are not allowed to watch the birth
65 of the baby. Each family must ask the doctor about the rules of
66 the hospital in which their child will be born. The doctor will try
67 to be helpful, but his first concern is the health of the child and
68 the mother.

11. According to the passage, the Caesarian section is used when
    (A) the mother is having twins
    (B) the father wants to watch the birth
    (C) the mother didn't exercise
    (D) the mother's pelvic area is too narrow
    (E) the mother wants to choose the date of birth

12. Write a definition of the term *prenatal care*
    _____

13. According to the author, natural and regular childbirth are different because
    (A) regular childbirth requires an operation
    (B) neither uses self-hypnosis for the delivery
    (C) natural childbirth is better
    (D) natural childbirth usually requires the use of medication
    (E) regular childbirth requires the use of medication

14. In lines 2-3, the author states that "the care she gives her unborn child is very important." From this we can infer that with prenatal care a baby will
    (A) weigh more
    (B) be happier
    (C) be healthier
    (D) have curly hair
    (E) be taller

15. Place a number on each line to show what the author suggests doing first (1), second (2), third (3), fourth (4) and last (5):
    ____ decide on the method of childbirth
    ____ see a doctor
    ____ find out about hospital rules concerning fathers
    ____ find out about prenatal care
    ____ deliver a healthy baby

4

Words You Need to Know

dimly   frail
agreement   volunteer

1   The hall outside of Apartment 301 was dimly lit. Tom
2   wasn't sure he wanted to get involved after all. "I wonder if this
3   is the right place," he thought. The rapping of his bare knuckles
4   echoed down the empty hallway.
5   The door swung open, and it was now too late to turn back.
6   "Come right in, I'm Frank Hall. You will meet the others in a
7   moment. Here, let me hang up your coat."
8   Tom followed the tall man into a bright room. It was a large
9   room with pieces of overstuffed furniture. The people sitting
10 around the room looked up to see the new member of the group.
11   "I want you to meet the others, young man. What is your
12 name, by the way."
13   "Tom, Tom Fox."
14   Everyone began introducing themselves.
15   "Sara here."
16   "Hi, I'm John."
17   "My name is Elaine."
18   "Rolly here, hello."
19   Tom quickly sat down in a maple chair. He gripped the
20 arms of the chair but barely noticed how his knuckles turned
21 white.

"Well, now that we are all here, I guess I can begin." The man speaking was Frank Hall, and the look on his face was hard to read. He began speaking very slowly, and he looked around at the sea of faces in the room. "You all know why you are here. We all know why we're meeting tonight in Apartment 301." All faces turned toward Frank and everyone listened carefully.

"Can I ask a question?" The voice was that of a frail, white-haired lady.

Tom tried to think of her name. "Betty, that's it, Betty," he remembered. She lived down the hall from him.

"Has everyone come here for the same reason?" she continued. "I don't think I really know why some of us have come. At least, I don't know if we all understand what we're trying to do."

Frank thought about that for a moment. "We all have to come to an agreement. Do you want to go around the room and have each person tell whether they are for or against us before we go on?"

Tom swallowed hard. No matter what he said, he would have to stick to his decision.

The group all sat around nodding in agreement to Frank's idea, and so it began.

Tom was last. He didn't volunteer any sooner than he had to, but now he had no choice.

"At first I thought it would be easier to move out. I wondered if it was worth the trouble to fight our landlord. But, if we all agree not to pay our rent, he can't throw us all out. It would cost him too much. Conditions in this building are worse than any other on the block. If we were animals, the anti-cruelty society would fight for us. But we are people, and we must fight for ourselves. We must all fight together, and I will do my part."

After Tom finished speaking, everyone clapped. People began to get up and walk around the room, promising one another to stand together against their landlord.

16. All of the people at the meeting have one thing in common. It is that
    (A) they all know Frank Hall
    (B) they all live in the same building
    (C) they all belong to the anti-cruelty society
    (D) they all can't pay their rent
    (E) they all work together

17. Right after Frank Hall welcomed him at the door, Tom
    (A) introduced himself
    (B) sat down in a maple chair
    (C) took off his coat
    (D) followed him into a large room
    (E) met Sara and John

18. In line 42 the words *stick* to his decision most nearly means
    (A) fight everyone else's decision
    (B) let someone change his mind about his decision
    (C) keep his word about his decision
    (D) uphold his right to make a decision
    (E) change his mind about his decision

19. The first two people that Tom met at the meeting were
    (A) John and Sara
    (B) Frank and John
    (C) Ellen and Frank
    (D) Elaine and John
    (E) Sara and Frank

20. When the author says, "the look on his face was hard to read" (lines 23-24), she means
    (A) Frank had something written on his forehead
    (B) Tom couldn't look at Frank
    (C) Frank had a funny-looking face
    (D) Tom couldn't tell what Frank was thinking
    (E) Frank was staring at him in a strange way

5

Words You Need to Know

lurching   slouched
bewildered   unconscious

1   When Joe Garra first moved to Auburn, on January 1, he
2 wanted to make friends and be part of what was happening in

3 town. But making friends had never been easy for Joe. He had
4 met a few people at work who seemed friendly. Tony Nichols
5 was one of the first people he met.
6   One night exactly two months after Joe had moved to
7 town, Tony called and said that he needed to talk to him. If Joe
8 would just meet him in front of the drugstore on Main Street in
9 a half hour, Tony would tell him about it. Twenty minutes later,
10 Joe wandered down Main Street in search of Tony.
11   "I wonder what's wrong with Tony," thought Joe. "It's one
12 o'clock in the morning and I'm not sure Tony's voice sounded
13 right on the telephone.
14   Tony was leaning against the corner of the drugstore
15 building. He was slouched over and had a crooked grin on his
16 face. "Hiya pal... Over here man, I'm over here," called Tony,
17 lurching forward toward a bewildered Joe. "Man, am I glad to
18 see you!" Tony's words were slurred as if he'd been drinking,
19 and he flung an arm around his newly arrived friend.
20   "Joe," Tony said, "I've just been in a car accident with the
21 company car. I totaled it! What's worse is that nobody knows
22 that I borrowed it for the evening. Do you know Sid Layden?
23 Well... the car's assigned to his department. If you could give
24 me some help getting the car off the street and over to..."
25   Before Tony could finish his sentence, he slid to the ground.
26 He looked unconscious. He wasn't moving, and Joe wasn't sure
27 if he was even breathing.
28   Joe looked down at Tony and said, "Hang on, old buddy.
29 I'll be right back." Joe moved quickly to the doorway of the
30 drugstore and slid into a nearby telephone booth. "Hello. It's
31 Joe from work. I need some help. Can you come to the drugstore
32 at Main and Grove?"
33   Joe hung up the phone and raced back to Tony. Tony had
34 crawled over to a fire hydrant and was trying to pull himself up
35 off the ground. Joe couldn't tell whether he was just drunk or he
36 had really been hurt in the accident.
37   Several minutes later, Sid Layden pulled his car up in front
38 of the drugstore. He was surprised to find out why Joe had
39 gotten him out of bed at this hour. Tony Nichols was the last
40 person Sid wanted to help. But the thought of letting Tony die
41 on the street wasn't pleasant either. No matter what Sid
42 thought of him, he could at least help get Tony to the hospital.
43 After that, he was someone else's problem.

44 After Joe and Sid got Tony to the hospital, the two of them
45 decided that a drink would be a good idea. Over drinks, Joe
46 asked, "Sid, why would Tony go off with a company car? Before
47 he passed out, Tony tried to say something. Do you know
48 what's going on?"
49 Sid swallowed hard, trying to decide whether he should tell
50 Joe what he thought of Tony. "Well," Sid began, "it isn't my
51 place to tell you about Tony's problem. If he wants you to know,
52 he'll tell you. All I can say is that some people prefer to mess up.
53 For them, no matter how good a situation is, they find some
54 way to ruin it for themselves. If they mess themselves up, they
55 won't give anyone else the chance to do them in."
56 It had been a long night. Joe thought about Tony and
57 decided that he didn't know what to think.

21. Joe had to fill out a police report when he took Tony to the hospital. Use the information from the passage to complete the report:

    Name _____

    Date _____

    Name of Accident Victim _____

    Time of Accident _____

    Place of Accident _____

    Owner of Vehicle _____

    Relationship to Victim _____

22. Joe called Sid Layden
    (A) before he met Tony
    (B) as soon as he saw Tony's condition
    (C) when Tony slid to the ground
    (D) as soon as he realized it was Sid's car
    (E) at 12:30 A.M.

23. Joe, Sid, and Tony
    (A) all held the same job
    (B) were the same age
    (C) were newcomers to town
    (D) worked for the same company
    (E) frequently went out together

24. Using the information in the passage about Tony and Sid, we can infer that
    (A) Tony is more successful than Sid
    (B) Sid is more successful than Tony
    (C) Tony and Sid have been good friends for a long time
    (D) Tony and Sid work in the same department
    (E) Tony doesn't like Sid

25. Sid wouldn't tell Joe much about Tony because
    (A) he didn't know much about him
    (B) he thought Joe would be shocked
    (C) he didn't think it was his place
    (D) he wanted to talk about something more interesting
    (E) he never talked about company men

ANSWERS AND EXPLANATIONS—UNIT IX

Seeing Relationships

1. (D) is the correct answer. This is a cause-effect relationship. Lines 8–10 state that the loss of a loved one can be the cause of a person's becoming depressed.

Seeing Relationships

2. (E) is the correct answer. In the last paragraph, the author states that a medical problem can be the *cause* of depression.

Finding the Main Idea

3. (A) is the best answer. The passage lists several of the causes of depression. There is no information to support answers (B), (C), or (D). Answer (E) only states one of the causes mentioned in the selection.

Seeing Relationships

4. (D) is the correct answer. The author is setting up a compare-contrast relationship. The author compares a cement block weighing down a person physically to depression weighing down a person's spirit.

Finding Supporting Details

5. You should have copied the last sentence of the fourth paragraph, lines 37–39. *"A large group of people at a party . . . may actually make that person more depressed."*

Making Inferences

6. (D) The carrots were the only item on Rose's menu that she didn't prepare herself. She had waited nervously all through dinner for his reaction so she probably felt a bit frustrated when he only made a joking comment about the carrots.

Making Inferences	7. **(D)**	is the best answer. Rose doesn't say anything to Abe about how excited she is to have his reaction until after the meal is over. You can infer that she hoped he would be fooled into thinking that this night was just like any other and then be surprised when he sat down to eat.
Making Inferences About Word Meaning	8. **(E)**	is the correct answer. You can infer the meaning of this word by noting that Abe didn't say anything during the meal.
Seeing Relationships	9. **(C)**	is the best answer. As a result of learning to cook, Rose is more confident (see lines 17-22). There is no information in the story to show that any of the other answer choices would be an effect of Rose's going to school.
Following Sequence	10. **(C)**	is the correct answer. In lines 25-26, the author states that the first thing Abe did was to give Rose a giant bear hug.
Finding Supporting Details	11. **(D)**	This fact is stated in lines 31-32.
Finding Supporting Details	12.	The term *prenatal care* describes everything done for a baby before its birth.
Finding Supporting Details	13. **(E)**	This fact is stated in lines 23-26.
Making Inferences	14. **(C)**	None of the specific characteristics listed in (A), (B), (D), and (E) are mentioned in the passage as a result of prenatal care. However, we can infer that the baby will be healthier when it's born if it was cared for properly before birth.

READING SELECTIONS 123

Following Sequence   15.   3, 1, 4, 2, 5

Seeing Relationships   16. **(B)** is the correct answer. From the last two paragraphs, you learn that they all have the same landlord and that they feel that they must stand together against him.

Following Sequence   17. **(C)** is the correct answer. From Frank's saying, "Here, let me hang up your coat" (line 7), you can conclude Tom took off his coat. All of the other events listed in the answer choices take place after this event.

Making Inferences About Word Meaning   18. **(C)** is the best answer. None of the other answers makes sense in the context of Tom's statement that follows.

Following Sequence   19. **(E)** is the correct answer. Since Frank answered the door and introduced himself, the correct answer has to include him. The first person to give her name (line 15) is Sara.

Making Inferences   20. **(D)** is the best answer. There is no support in the passage for (A) or (C). (E) is false since lines 24-25 state that he looked around the room at everyone; so he couldn't have been staring at Tom. (B) is false since Tom must be looking at Frank to notice the expression on his face.

Following Directions   21.   Name   <u>Joe Garra</u>

    Date   <u>March 1</u>

    Name of Accident Victim   <u>Tony Nichols</u>

    Time of Accident   <u>about 1:00 A.M.</u>

124 READING SELECTIONS

Place of Accident   <u>near drugstore at the corner of Main and Grove</u>

Owner of Vehicle   <u>company vehicle assigned to Sid Layden</u>

Relationship to Victim   <u>work together</u>

Following Sequence

22. **(C)** Joe didn't call Sid until Tony passed out (see lines 25–39).

Seeing Relationships

23. **(D)** There is no support in the passage for (A), (B), or (E). Only Joe is a newcomer to the town, according to the passage, so (C) is also unsupported. We do know that Joe and Tony work together (lines 4–5) and we find out in lines 22–23 that Sid works for the same company.

Making Inferences

24. **(B)** According to lines 39–40, Sid doesn't like Tony, so (C) is false. Line 23 states that the car that Tony took was assigned to Sid's department so that we can infer that they don't work in the same department (D). There is no support for (E). Since Sid describes Tony as someone who always messes up (lines 50–55), it is safe to conclude that Tony is not more successful than Sid (A).

Finding Supporting Details

25. **(C)** This fact is stated in lines 50–51.

UNIT IX: READING SELECTIONS—EVALUATION CHART

In order to see how well you've done on the Unit IX Reading Selections, see which questions you got right and which ones you got wrong. Then check against the chart below to find out which, if any types of questions gave you trouble.

Circle the numbers of the questions you got right in the chart below. Enter the number of right answers of each type and the total.

Reading Skill	Question Numbers	Number of Correct Answers	Study Pages
Finding the Main Idea	3		19-26
Finding Supporting Details	5, 11, 12, 13, 25		20-23
Making Inferences	6, 7, 14, 20, 24		37-42
Making Inferences About Word Meaning	8, 18		173-181
Seeing Relationships	1, 2, 4, 9, 16, 23		85-93
Following Sequence	10, 15, 17, 19, 22		29-34
Following Directions	21		77-82

Total number of correct answers _____

UNIT X: DRAWING CONCLUSIONS

(1) Fred gets drunk after two beers.
(2) Fred just finished his third beer.
(3) Therefore, _____

Can you fill in the blank to complete the third sentence? To get the correct answer, you must *draw a conclusion* based on the information given in the first two sentences. You can only conclude that *Fred is drunk*.

Drawing a conclusion is simply a matter of putting facts together. In the following exercise, there is only one way to put the facts together to draw a conclusion.

Exercise A

DIRECTIONS: Using the facts given in the first two sentences in each of the groups of sentences below, you will be able to draw a conclusion. Finish the third sentence in each group by writing your conclusion. Check your answers in the Answer Key at the end of the unit.

1. (A) If a person has a temperature over 100°, he probably has some kind of infection.
   (B) I have a temperature of 102°.
   (C) Therefore, _____

2. (A) There is no heat in my apartment.
   (B) Whenever I forget to pay the gas bill, the gas company turns off my heat.
   (C) Therefore, _____

3. (A) Caffeine helps to keep you awake.
   (B) Coffee contains caffeine.
   (C) Therefore, _____

4. (A) I have a pain in my back.
   (B) Whenever I have a pain in my back, I know it is going to rain.
   (C) Therefore, _____

5. (A) Eating chili peppers always gives me heartburn.
   (B) I just ate a taco with lots of chili peppers on it.
   (C) Therefore, _____

6. (A) I just saw Henry go into the garage.
   (B) The only time Henry goes to the garage is when he and Loretta have had a fight.
   (C) Therefore, _____

Whenever you read, you gather facts and ideas, often without even thinking about it. You then draw conclusions based on what you gathered while reading, adding what you already know about life.

A writer doesn't always spell out the facts as clearly as in Exercise A. You may be expected to pick up clues about the facts based on the writer's choice of words. If the writer wants you to draw a particular conclusion, he will choose his words carefully.

In the following exercise, you will be able to draw a conclusion by paying careful attention to the clues in the words the writer uses.

Exercise B

DIRECTIONS: Read each item below. You will be asked to draw a conclusion based on what you read. Check your answers in the Answer Key at the end of the unit.

1. The donkey climbed slowly under the heavy weight of the burden it was carrying. With each step it took, more pebbles fell down to the ground below.

   The donkey is
   (A) at the beach.
   (B) on a mountain side.
   (C) walking in the woods.

2. The sun was coming up. The air smelled clean and fresh from last night's heavy rain. The grass glistened with dew.

   The time of day is
   (A) afternoon.
   (B) early morning.
   (C) late evening.

DRAWING CONCLUSIONS   129

3. Eight men had been sharing food that would have been enough for only three men. This was all the food they could save when the boat overturned. Now all the food was gone. The men sat there barely moving, wondering if help would come in time.

   The men are
   - (A) taking a break on the trail.
   - (B) faint from hunger.
   - (C) getting ready to go fishing.

4. Ron continued to drive through the night. The blizzard was making the driving very hard. He thought about stopping for the night at a motel. Then he remembered his promise to his daughter Jennifer. Tomorrow would be her birthday, and he had promised to be home when she woke up in the morning.

   Ron was
   - (A) determined to be home by morning.
   - (B) unable to continue driving in the snow.
   - (C) running out of gas.

5. Stan lay in a heap on the ground. He had been warned many times to wear his safety equipment, but he claimed that it only got in his way. He felt free and alive atop the telephone pole, looking down at the world as he repaired the lines. Now, he was free forever.

   Stan
   - (A) fell off a telephone pole and died.
   - (B) tripped and hurt himself.
   - (C) just quit his job.

6. The bears ate the last of the jam sandwiches, walked away from the car, and lay down to sleep.

   The bears now feel
   - (A) playful.
   - (B) hungry.
   - (C) contented.

7. The lioness moved slowly. She had escaped from the circus last night. She was crouching as she walked, seeming to know the streets would be filled with men trying to recapture her.

The lioness was
- (A) hiding out.
- (B) feeling lazy.
- (C) moving carefully.

In the two exercises you have done in this unit, you were able to draw a conclusion based on clear facts. Sometimes, however, there are many ways of putting the facts together. Depending on how you put the facts together, and depending on your own experiences in life, you may be able to draw several different conclusions.

Sometimes you may not be able to find clear facts on which to draw a conclusion. Read the following paragraph and try to complete the sentence that follows the paragraph.

> It's 5 P.M. and you're waiting. You know you love him and he feels the same way. Today is the day he'll be visiting Chicago. He said he'd call just as soon as he got into town. That was four days ago. Is he all right? Has he been in an accident? Were the telephone lines jammed? Could he have forgotten? Perhaps he really doesn't care after all. There's nothing to do but wait . . . and hope . . . and . . . *RING!* His greeting, "Hello, darling," instantly changes your mood.

From what you just read, you might conclude that the person for whom the woman is waiting

- (A) doesn't keep track of time.
- (B) had no change for a telephone call.
- (C) was delayed and probably tried to call.
- (D) called just as soon as he arrived.
- (E) (fill in your own conclusion) _____

There is no *right* conclusion you can draw. There are not enough facts given in the paragraph to make one of the conclusions above better than the others. All of the conclusions are possible. There are many possible explanations for someone to call later than you expected or hoped.

DRAWING CONCLUSIONS

The key word here is *possible*. Whatever conclusion you draw, it must be possible. In Exercise A, you put two facts together to draw the only possible conclusion. In Exercise B, you took a close look at the words a writer used to find out what conclusions were impossible and what conclusion was possible. In both Exercise A and Exercise B, you were able to draw only one possible conclusion.

Now, read the paragraph below. Which of the conclusions that follow the paragraph are possible?

> It's 5 P.M. and you're waiting. You know you love him and he feels the same way. Today is the day he'll be visiting Chicago. He said he'd call just as soon as he got into town. That was four days ago. Is he all right? Has he been in an accident? Were the telephone lines jammed? Could he have forgotten? Perhaps he really doesn't care after all. There's nothing to do but wait . . . and hope . . . and . . . wonder if he'll ever call.

From this paragraph, you might conclude that the person who is waiting for the phone call

(A) is upset.
(B) is afraid that the man will never call.
(C) is calmly waiting for the phone to ring.
(D) just met the man the night before.

Both (A) and (B) are possible conclusions. There is nothing in the paragraph to prove either of these conclusions wrong. At the same time, there is nothing in the paragraph to lead you to draw either conclusion (C) or conclusion (D). The fact that the person is worrying about what could have kept the man from calling does not show that the person is *calmly* waiting. The fact that the man told the person that he would call *four days ago* proves that conclusion (D) is wrong.

Whatever conclusion you draw, that conclusion must be supported by facts. As you read, you will discover several different facts. When you put them together to draw your conclusion, you must make sure that none of the facts proves your conclusion wrong.

132 DRAWING CONCLUSIONS

Exercise C

DIRECTIONS: Read the following short story. There is no ending, or conclusion, to the story. Based on the facts you find in the story, write an ending. There is no one right conclusion to the story, but whatever conclusion you draw must be based on the facts. Several possible conclusions are given in the Answer Key at the end of the unit.

1 Sam was having a bad day. He'd cut himself shaving that
2 morning. He was late for work. And to make matters worse,
3 when he finally left home, he'd locked the door and left his keys
4 on the dresser.

5 The morning newspaper didn't make the day seem any
6 better. On the front page was another story about the mad
7 killer. The police had been unable to find the killer, and now,
8 another woman in Sam's neighborhood had been murdered.
9 Sam had put two new locks on the door to his apartment, but he
10 still worried about Irene.

11 It was 6:15 when Sam returned home. No one answered
12 the door. Annoyed, he muttered under his breath, "Where is
13 Irene? She should have been home hours ago." Sam went
14 around to the back of the building and discovered that the
15 bedroom window was partly open. He pried the window com-
16 pletely open and crawled over the dusty sill.

17 By now, his temper was getting out of control. As he spoke
18 aloud to no one but the four walls, the sound of his voice was
19 frightening. "I've told that woman she's supposed to be home
20 when I get home from work. That's all I ever ask. She can't
21 seem to do one simple thing. Well, I've had it! Tonight we're
22 going to talk, and I mean *talk*. I've had about all of her non-
23 sense that I'll put up with. DAMN!" Sam had hit his head on
24 the bedroom door. That did nothing to calm him down. He pro-
25 ceeded in rage to the kitchen.

26 Sam stopped in the doorway. After a few moments of look-
27 ing at the scene he'd found, he began to moan. He held his head
28 in his hands and began to sob hysterically. The sight before
29 him was not pretty. Irene lay on her side in a pool of blood, the
30 handle of a kitchen knife showing from her chest.

"Oh, my God!" The cry that came from Sam's throat was like a wail. He stumbled over to where her body lay, knelt down, and gathered her up in his arms. "Irene, Irene. . ." Sobs choked off the words.

When the police burst into the room, Sam was startled. Mrs. Blake, the upstairs neighbor, had called the police when she heard Sam's screams. Sam was immediately taken to the police station for questioning.

Sam tried to explain what had happened. This was not the first time that the police had been called to Sam's apartment. They simply didn't believe his story. Sam was charged with murder and held over for trial.

A number of confusing facts came out at the trial. The time of death was fixed at 4:00. Two of Sam's fellow workers testified that Sam had disappeared from work about 3:00. Sam claimed that he was running an errand for his boss, but he couldn't prove where he was at 4:00.

Mrs. Blake told the jury about Sam's violent temper. There had been many evenings on which she had had to call the police to restore the peace. Irene had told Mrs. Blake on the morning of the murder that she was worried about Sam's behavior.

The family doctor was called to the witness stand. He knew that Sam was distressed, but he didn't think that Sam was capable of killing anyone. The doctor did know something important that he thought he should mention. Irene was dying of cancer. She hadn't told Sam about it yet; she had only been told about it herself on the morning of the murder. The doctor testified that Irene was understandably upset about the news. "Before she left my office at 2:30, she said, 'I'd rather just die now than have to tell Sam,'" the doctor said.

The last person to testify was Inspector Kelly. "I have solved the case. . . ."

Exercise D

DIRECTIONS: Read the short story below. Again, there is no ending, or conclusion, to the story. Based on the facts you find in the story, write a conclusion. There is no one right conclusion to the story, but whatever conclusion you draw must be based on the facts. Several possible conclusions are given in the Answer Key at the end of the unit.

1 Lynn Tanner sat in her father's favorite chair. She closed
2 her eyes. It had been more than sixteen years since she'd been
3 in this old house. Since running away at seventeen, she had
4 crossed the United States. She had never once had the urge to
5 return. Not even when Howard, her older brother, sent the tele-
6 gram to say that her folks had died in an automobile accident.
7 It was difficult to feel grief for a family that hadn't spoken to
8 her for sixteen years. When her father had married Sara after
9 the death of his first wife, Lynn's mother, things had changed.
10 Sara made it quite clear that she didn't care for Lynn. It was
11 Sara who turned her husband against his only daughter.

12 Lynn thought back to the summer she had left. "I was
13 seventeen and pregnant by a boy who refused to marry me,"
14 Lynn thought to herself. "Did I get any help from my family?
15 You bet I didn't! It's been hard, but I've managed. I probably
16 made Sara very happy when I ran away."

17 Now, eight months after her father's and stepmother's
18 deaths, the family had been gathered to hear the will. Although
19 Lynn wanted no part of anything left by her father, she'd come
20 out of a sense of loyalty to Howard and out of her own curiosity.

21 Lynn looked around the room. There was Louise, Howard's
22 wife. Louise was sitting on the sofa with a funny smile on her
23 face. For years after Lynn had run off, Louise had looked after
24 the house and had waited hand and foot on Howard's father
25 and stepmother. Now, at last, she was probably thinking, she
26 was going to get her reward for all the sacrifices she had made
27 for Howard and his parents. Lynn loved her brother too much
28 to say anything against Louise, but she was certain that How-
29 ard could have found a more charming wife.

30 John, Junior, Lynn's oldest brother, gripped the arms of
31 his chair. He resented Louise for being so demanding of How-
32 ard.

Mr. Hall, the lawyer, walked into the room. He looked hot and tired. He asked Louise for a glass of water. The lawyer stood before the three children of John Tanner, Senior. He pulled at his collar in a gesture that indicated that his tie was too tight and that he was feeling uncomfortable at the moment. He cleared his throat.

"The document I am about to read is the last will and testament that was drawn up in my office two years before the deaths of John and Sara Tanner. As you know, there were some legal claims on the Tanner property that kept my office from presenting the will before now. I want to explain that it was your father's wish that whatever he had to give should not be divided up. He also wanted me to explain to you that he wanted everything to go where it was most needed and deserved. Now that I have said that, let me read the will."

When the reading of the will was finished, silence filled the room.

ANSWER KEY—UNIT X

Exercise A

1. Therefore, I probably have some kind of infection.
2. Therefore, I forgot to pay the gas bill.
3. Therefore, coffee helps to keep you awake.
4. Therefore, I know it is going to rain.
5. Therefore, the taco is going to give me heartburn.
6. Therefore, Henry and Loretta have had a fight.

Exercise B

1. (B) on a mountain side

    You can draw this conclusion by noting that the donkey is *climbing* and that the pebbles are falling *down*.

2. (B) early morning

    You can drawn this conclusion by noting that the sun *comes up* in the morning and that *dew* is usually found in the morning.

3. (B) faint from hunger

    You can draw this conclusion based on the facts that (1) all the food is gone, (2) the men are barely moving, and (3) the men are not sure that they will be saved.

4. (A) determined to be home by morning

    You can draw this conclusion by putting together the first and last sentences. "Ron *continued* to drive . . ." and "he had promised to be home when she woke up *in the morning.*"

5. (A) fell off a telephone pole and died

    You can draw this conclusion by noting that Stan's job requires him to climb telephone poles and that he refuses to wear safety equipment. If Stan is "free forever," and if he is lying "in a heap on the ground," he must be dead and he must have fallen.

138   DRAWING CONCLUSIONS

6. (C) contented

    You can draw this conclusion by noting that the bears have just eaten (therefore they cannot be *B. hungry)* and that they are going to sleep (therefore they cannot be *A. playful).* You can also apply the knowledge that bears, like humans, usually rest after they are full and content.

7. (C) moving carefully

    You can draw this conclusion by noting the words *moved slowly* and *crouching as she walked.* The lioness cannot be hiding if she is moving. She also cannot be feeling lazy; if she were feeling lazy, she would most likely be lying down somewhere.

Exercise C

Any of the following conclusions are possible based on the facts in the story. Depending on which conclusion you drew, check to see that you supported it with the facts given in the answers below.

(1) Although everyone had a reason to kill Irene, the real killer is the "mad killer" in the newspaper story (mentioned in lines 6-8).

(2) Sam killed Irene. He has a violent temper (mentioned in line 48 and demonstrated in lines 12-25). Even though he didn't have his keys, remember that the bedroom window was open.

(3) Irene killed herself. Irene knew she was dying of cancer, and she preferred to die quickly rather than slowly and painfully. This would also explain her remark to the doctor in lines 60-61.

Exercise D

Any of the following conclusions are possible based on the facts in the story. Remember that all of the property and money can only go to one person(lines 47-50). Depending on which conclusion you drew, check to see that you supported it with the facts given in the answers below.

(1) Lynn got everything. The Tanners felt sorry for what had happened when Lynn was seventeen(see lines 7-16). Since they had given her little in life, they wanted to give her something after death. They knew that life had been hard for Lynn and were at last giving her a break. In order to think that Lynn was the person who "most needed and deserved" the money, they must reject their two sons. They could see through Louise, and they decided that they had given Howard and Louise enough already.

(2) Howard and Louise got everything. They had stayed with the Tanners and taken care of them (lines 23-26). This was the Tanners' way of rewarding them.

(3) John, Junior, got everything. He was the oldest child, and the Tanners felt that he would accept responsibility for the rest of the family.

(4) Everything went to charity, and none of the children got anything. The Tanners felt that their children could take care of themselves and wanted to help people who really needed and deserved the money.

(5) There was nothing left to give to anyone. The "legal claims on the Tanner property" mentioned in line 46 took up all the money the Tanners had.

UNIT XI: UNDERSTANDING FIGURATIVE LANGUAGE

If someone wants to be left alone, that person can say either

"Leave me alone"   **or**   "Get lost"

"Leave me alone" gives you a clear, direct message. The statement means exactly what it says. *"Get lost"* is a more forceful way of saying the same thing. For speakers of American English, *"Get lost"* is understood to mean the same thing as *"Leave me alone"*; we know that we are not really being told to go somewhere where we will be lost.

When language is used to have a meaning other than the usual meaning of the words (as in *"Get lost"*), it is called **figurative language.** This figurative language helps the reader share the writer's feeling.

You can understand the sentence below simply by knowing the meaning of each word in the sentence:

Mary looked beautiful at the party last night.

But, let's suppose you read:

Mary really knocked me out at the party last night.

To understand this sentence, you need to know more than the meaning of each word.

First, you must find out whether the writer is using the words with their usual meanings or whether the writer is using the words with a figurative meaning. Does the writer mean that Mary slugged him and "knocked him out"? In order to know whether the writer is using words with their usual meanings, you must know the general situation the writer is talking about. This is sometimes called the **context** in which the words are used. You can find the context of a writer's statement by reading the sentences that come before or after the sentence in which the puzzling words appear. Look at the sample sentence in the following two contexts:

(1) Mary really knocked me out at the party last night. I must have said something nasty, so she hit me.

(2) Mary really knocked me out at the party last night. I have never seen her looking so beautiful before.

In each of these two examples, the second sentence tells you what the writer is talking about; that is, the second sentence gives you the context in which the first sentence is written.

In the first example, the writer is describing the effect of Mary's hitting him. In the first example, then, the writer is using the words *knocked me out* with their usual meaning. In the second example, however, the words *knocked me out* do not mean the same thing at all. In the second example, the writer is describing the effect of Mary's beauty.

If you know that *knocked me out* can be used with the meaning *to have a strong positive effect on someone,* you know without thinking what the writer means. If you don't already know the figurative meaning of *knocked me out,* you can figure it out from the context. In this example, Mary's beauty is so powerful that it is like getting hit; the writer was so stunned when he saw Mary that he felt just as if she had hit him. You can almost see the writer falling back against a wall, letting his mouth fall open, to let Mary know that he thinks she is truly beautiful.

In this unit, you will take a close look at several different types of figurative language. Once you become aware of this use of language, it will be much easier for you to understand what writers are saying.

You have already looked at one of the most common uses of figurative language. Both *"Get lost"* and *"Mary really knocked me out at the party last night"* use words with a figurative meaning. There are many groups of words that we use or hear every day that make sense only if we know the figurative meaning. For example, *"Don't cry over spilt milk"* is said at a time when there are no tears or milk in sight. You know that this statement doesn't make sense if you depend upon the dictionary definition of each word. However, you do know that it is easier to wipe up milk that has been spilled than it is to try to get it back into a glass. It is because of this fact that this statement is used to mean that *"it is easier to forget than to worry about a hopeless situation."*

Because *"Don't cry over spilt milk"* is used so often, you are probably already familiar with its figurative meaning. In the following exercise, you will find other groups of words that are frequently used with a figurative meaning. Even if you are not already familiar with some of them, you should be able to find the meaning from the context.

UNDERSTANDING FIGURATIVE LANGUAGE

Exercise A

DIRECTIONS: The sentences below include words that have a figurative meaning. Underline these words in each sentence. Then select from the list below the clear meaning of the words. Write the letter of the correct answer in the space provided. Check your answers in the Answer Key at the end of the unit.

(A) is very clumsy
(B) raining very hard
(C) trying to trick me
(D) received loud applause from the listeners
(E) told the secret by accident
(F) to get me to do whatever she wants me to do
(G) write me a letter
(H) extremely delighted
(I) just barely
(J) has a special talent for growing plants

_____ 1. My sister's garden is always fantastic because she has a green thumb.

_____ 2. Did you really mean that or are you pulling my leg?

_____ 3. I already know about that. Jean let the cat out of the bag.

_____ 4. After you've lived there a while, please drop a line.

_____ 5. When I left this morning, it was sunny but now it's pouring cats and dogs.

_____ 6. I don't like to dance with Paul. He has two left feet.

_____ 7. After Maria was awarded the prize for being the most valuable basketball player, she was walking on air.

_____ 8. I plan to do it my own way, but whenever I drop over to visit my mother, she manages to wind me around her little finger.

_____ 9. I escaped being hurt by the skin of my teeth.

_____ 10. David got a big hand when he finished telling his story to that group of ex-employees.

UNDERSTANDING FIGURATIVE LANGUAGE

Look at the following sentence, paying special attention to the words that are used with a figurative meaning.

Jason's sadness weighs on him like a cement block.

Although there are no cement blocks on Jason's body, someone who is sad usually has the posture and the walk of a person carrying a heavy burden. The words *like a cement block* are being used with a figurative meaning. It might have been simpler to write *"Jason is sad."* Both *"Jason is sad"* and *"Jason's sadness weighs on him like a cement block"* express sadness. However, *"Jason is sad"* does not tell the reader how sad Jason is. By comparing Jason's sadness to the weight of a cement block, the writer has been able to give his reader a better idea of just how sad Jason is.

When a writer compares two different or unrelated things to show that they have something in common, he is using a type of figurative language known as a **simile**. Just think of the word *similar*. A simile uses the words *like* or *as* to show the comparison. These are your clues! Writers use similes to make a strong point, to emphasize an idea, and to make their writing more interesting.

If a writer says, "Paul is as old-fashioned as motherhood and apple pie," he is comparing Paul to motherhood and apple pie—both are old-fashioned. The writer's statement is a simile; Paul is described by comparing him to something that has a similar quality. In the following exercise, all of the similes are used to describe someone or something in terms of a quality of something else.

Exercise B

DIRECTIONS: Complete the nine similes below by using one of the words given in the list. Each word is used only once. Check your answers in the Answer Key at the end of the unit.

snail   log
wet match firecracker
thread   horse
elephant mule
glue

UNDERSTANDING FIGURATIVE LANGUAGE

1. Sara is as thin as a (an) _____
2. Greta has a memory like a (an) _____
3. Our waiter last night was as slow as a (an) _____
4. The muffler on my car is as noisy as a (an) _____
5. Waitress, my coffee cup has a hole in the bottom; it's as useless as a (an) _____
6. You'll never get Frank to go to Linda's party. When it comes to going someplace he doesn't want to go to, he can be as stubborn as a (an) _____
7. Shirley left her lollipop on the table, and now the table top is as sticky as _____
8. I was so tired last night that I slept like a (an) _____
9. No wonder Gloria is so fat; she eats like a (an) _____

A simile can be used to express or create a special mood. In the following exercise, the same thing is described by using four different similes. The different similes create different moods.

Exercise C

DIRECTIONS: In each of these sentences about the wind, a different simile is used. From the list below, choose the mood that the simile is trying to create. Write the letter of the correct answer in the space next to the sentence. Check your answers in the Answer Key at the end of the unit.

(A) playful
(B) quiet
(C) soft
(D) fierce

_____ 1. The wind is like a whisper in a dark room.
_____ 2. The wind is like a bull that has been injured or teased.

_____ 3. The wind is like a lake settling after the swimmers have finally gone home.

_____ 4. The wind is like a kitten with a fluffy ball of yarn.

A writer may make a comparison between two different things without using the words *like* or *as*. For example, a writer might say, *"Mac is a pig at the table,"* instead of saying, *"Mac is a sloppy eater."* The writer is talking about a person named Mac, not about an animal (a pig) named Mac. By saying that *"Mac is a pig,"* he is pointing out Mac's poor table manners by comparing Mac to a pig. Mac and a pig do have something in common—they are both sloppy eaters.

A comparison between two different things that does not use the words *like* or *as* is called a **metaphor**. The difference between a simile and a metaphor is that similes use the words *like* or *as* and metaphors do not. The sentence *"Mac is a pig at the table"* uses a metaphor. When a writer uses a metaphor, he depends upon your knowing about one person or thing (in this case, a pig) in order to understand something about a person or thing that you don't know (in this case, Mac). Your understanding of the usual meaning of a word (such as *pig*) will help you understand the figurative meaning of that same word *(pig* means *sloppy eater)*. In the following exercise, six common words are used in metaphors. If you think about the usual meanings of the words, you will be able to understand the writer's metaphor.

Exercise D

DIRECTIONS: Each of the following sentences contains a metaphor. Underline the word that has a figurative meaning in the metaphor. In the blank next to each sentence write the letter of the definition of the figurative meaning. Check your answers in the Answer Key at the end of the unit.

(A) someone who is very aggressive, forceful, and energetic
(B) someone who is grouchy and irritable
(C) someone who lets someone or something else control his life
(D) something that tastes awful
(E) something strong enough to knock you out
(F) someone or something powerful and evil

UNDERSTANDING FIGURATIVE LANGUAGE

_____ 1. Susan is a slave to her job.

_____ 2. This coffee is poison.

_____ 3. Alex's vodka punch is a killer.

_____ 4. Peg is a tiger on the basketball court.

_____ 5. The political bosses in this city are monsters.

_____ 6. I am a bear when I first get up in the morning.

One special kind of metaphor is called **personification**. The key here is the word *person*. The following sentence is an example of personification:

The sun smiled on the world today.

The writer describes an action of the sun as though the sun were a person. Of course, the sun cannot actually smile as a person does. The writer is drawing on your feelings about smiling to create a certain effect. A person's smile is an expression of a bright, cheerful attitude. For most people, this same feeling of cheerfulness is created by a bright sun in a clear, blue sky. Although the writer has described the sun as if it were a person, we understand that *"the sun smiled"* means *"the sun was shining brightly."*

Just as a metaphor uses a common word to express a shared quality between two things or between a person and a thing, personification uses words that are usually used to describe people to describe a quality of a nonliving thing. In the following exercise, you will be given a chance to use personification. Notice how the use of personification spices up the original sentences.

148 UNDERSTANDING FIGURATIVE LANGUAGE

Exercise E

DIRECTIONS: In each of the following sentences, one part of the sentence has been underlined. From the three choices given after each sentence, choose the one that uses personification to express the same meaning as the underlined part. Write the letter of the correct answer in the blank next to the sentence. Check your answers in the Answer Key at the end of the unit.

_____ 1. The wind is not very strong.

  (A) is barely moving the leaves on the trees
  (B) kissed our cheeks
  (C) slapped us in the face

_____ 2. The waves were high due to the storm.

  (A) were angry
  (B) were like glass
  (C) were immense

_____ 3. The mountains rise far above the sea.

  (A) are high above
  (B) looked down on
  (C) looked up from

_____ 4. My car uses a lot of gas.

  (A) sips
  (B) chews up
  (C) guzzles

_____ 5. Your car sounds as if it is ready for the scrap heap.

  (A) going to lie down and die
  (B) going to take off without you
  (C) having mechanical difficulty

_____ 6. My job is very hard for me.

  (A) killing me
  (B) extremely difficult for me
  (C) like hell on earth

UNDERSTANDING FIGURATIVE LANGUAGE

Have you ever found yourself saying, "I wish I could find the words to express how I feel"? For example, when a relative dies, it seems too weak just to say "I feel sad." Or when (and if) you find that special someone, it just isn't enough to say, "You make me feel so happy." Words like *sad* and *happy* just don't express how you feel.

Writers have this same problem every time they try to describe a person, or a place, or a feeling. In order to give their readers an idea of what the writer sees or what the writer feels, writers use figurative expressions like those you have been studying in this unit. Using similes, metaphors, and personification helps the writer say what he wants to say in a more precise way.

In the following exercise, you will read a description of something that happened to a writer. The writer could have told you what happened in two sentences, but instead, he uses figurative language to try to describe just how he felt.

Exercise F

DIRECTIONS: Read the following paragraph, and then answer the questions that follow the paragraph. Circle the letters of the correct answers. Check your answers in the Answer Key at the end of the unit.

1 I had waited all day for this moment, like a child waiting to
2 go to the circus. I turned on the television and settled into my
3 favorite chair. But, the television is a cruel dictator. It
4 demanded that I first swallow the bitter medicine called a com-
5 mercial. As the commercial ended, I sat up straight, eagerly
6 waiting for the beginning of my program. Suddenly, like a
7 spoiled brat, the set began making faces at me. The bright,
8 clear picture of the commercial became a lot of jagged lines. I
9 got up to adjust the knobs, pleading with this spoiled child to
10 behave. It responded with even worse faces. I became a soldier,
11 ready to do battle with my enemy. I doubled up my fist and
12 pounded the set firmly on its head. It let out a shriek from the
13 pain. I pounded it again, and it began making sounds like a cat
14 trying to frighten its attacker. At last, worn out from playing its
15 game, it suddenly stopped. It just sat there with a blank stare
16 on its face, stubbornly refusing to play with me anymore. I
17 slumped to the floor, feeling like a child who was being unfairly
18 punished for something he didn't do. I couldn't argue or fight; I
19 had to give up and accept what the TV had done to me.

150 UNDERSTANDING FIGURATIVE LANGUAGE

1. When the writer says that he was "like a child waiting to go to the circus" (lines 1-2), he means that he was

   (A) going to watch a circus on television
   (B) excited about seeing something he had been waiting for
   (C) not looking forward to something he knew was going to happen

2. The television is called "a cruel dictator" (line 3) because

   (A) the writer has no control over what is shown on television
   (B) the writer is forced to sit and watch it
   (C) the writer doesn't like television

3. "The set began making faces at me" (line 7) means that

   (A) there was a picture of a face on the set
   (B) the picture was ruined by a lot of lines
   (C) the set went off

4. When the writer says that he "became a soldier" (line 10), he means that

   (A) he was dressed up like a soldier
   (B) he had fought many battles with television
   (C) he was fighting mad

5. "It just sat there with a blank stare on its face" (lines 15-16) means

   (A) the picture went off completely
   (B) the picture became nothing more than a lot of lines
   (C) the picture never changed

6. Both at the beginning and at the end of the story, the writer uses a simile involving a child. This is probably because

   (A) the writer is a child
   (B) the writer feels as helpless as a child
   (C) the writer never really grew up

UNDERSTANDING FIGURATIVE LANGUAGE

ANSWER KEY—UNIT XI

Exercise A

Only the words you should have underlined are given below.

- J 1. has a green thumb
- C 2. pulling my leg
- E 3. let the cat out of the bag
- G 4. drop a line
- B 5. pouring cats and dogs
- A 6. has two left feet
- H 7. walking on air
- F 8. to wind me around her little finger
- I 9. by the skin of my teeth
- D 10. got a big hand

Exercise B

1. thin as a thread
2. memory like an elephant
3. slow as a snail
4. noisy as a firecracker
5. useless as a wet match
6. stubborn as a mule
7. sticky as glue
8. slept like a log
9. eats like a horse

Exercise C

1. (C) soft
2. (D) fierce
3. (B) quiet
4. (A) playful

Exercise D

The words you should have underlined are set in boldface type.

1. (C) A **slave** is someone who lets someone or something else control his life.
2. (D) Something that is described as **poison** is something that tastes awful.
3. (E) Something that is described as a **killer** is something that is strong enough to knock you out.
4. (A) A **tiger** is someone who is very aggressive, forceful, and energetic.
5. (F) A **monster** is someone or something powerful and evil.
6. (B) A **bear** is someone who is grouchy and irritable.

Exercise E

1. (B) kissed our cheeks

    Choice (A) is not an example of personification. Choice (C) implies that the wind is strong. Only choice (B) has a meaning that implies gentleness.

2. (A) were angry

    Choice (B) is a simile that would mean that the waves were smooth, not at all like waves in a storm. Choice (C) is not an example of personification. Saying that the waves were angry implies that they were large and powerful.

3. (B) looked down on

    Choice (A) is not an example of personification. Choice (C) implies that the mountains were lower than the sea if they have to look up to see the sea. Only choice (B) carries the meaning of rising far above the sea; if the mountains had eyes, they would have to look down to see the sea.

4. (C) guzzles

    Choice (A) carries a meaning of taking only a little; when a person sips a drink, he drinks very little at a time. Choice (B) would be all right if gas were solid, but gas is liquid; a person does not chew on something liquid. Only choice (C) carries the meaning of taking in a lot of liquid.

5. (A) going to lie down and die

Choice (B) implies that the car still is in good condition. Choice (C) is not an example of personification. Only choice (B) implies that the car is in terrible condition and ready to be sold for scrap.

6. (A) killing me

Choice (B) is not an example of personification. Choice (C) is a simile comparing working the job to living in hell; the job is not given any quality of a person. Only choice (A) describes the job as performing an action that only people can do (killing).

Exercise F

1. (B) excited about seeing something he had been waiting for

This is a simile. The writer is describing his own feeling of excitement and anticipation as being *like* a child's excitement about going to see a circus. He does not really mean that he, the writer, is going to see a circus; therefore, choice (A) is incorrect. Choice (C) is also incorrect; very few children would *not* look forward to seeing a circus.

2. (A) the writer has no control over what is shown on television

This is a metaphor. A dictator tells people what they will do, and the people have no control over the dictator. In the same way, individual television viewers have no control over what is shown on television. However, people do have the choice not to watch any television if they don't want to watch it. The writer is not being forced to watch; the television doesn't have that much control. Therefore, choice (B) is not correct. Choice (C) is also not true; the writer would like very much to see a certain program, the one he has been waiting all day to watch.

3. (B) the picture was ruined by a lot of lines

The sentence just after this example of personification (lines 7-8) explains what the writer means by "faces."

4. (C) he was fighting mad

This is a metaphor. The writer is not really a soldier, nor is he dressed up as a soldier. As the sentence that follows this metaphor explains, the writer hits the television set just as a soldier might attack an enemy. Although it is quite likely that the writer has done this before, the writer does not say that this is true; therefore, choice (B) is incorrect.

5. (A) the picture went off completely

This is another example of personification. The *face* of a television would be the picture tube, and a *blank stare* would be no picture at all. When a person gives you a blank stare, he reveals no emotion or clue to what he is thinking. If a television could be described as giving someone a blank stare, it would mean about the same thing—the television shows nothing at all.

6. (B) the writer feels as helpless as a child

The writing alone should tell you that the writer is not really a child. However, like a child, the writer feels unable to do what he wants to do because of something outside his control.

UNIT XII: INTERPRETING IMAGERY

What's wrong with this picture?

The woman in this picture looks out of place. She's dressed as a bride and seems very happy. Close your eyes for a moment and picture any bride you've seen. What kind of mental picture, or **image**, did you see? Whatever your answer, it is not very likely that you saw that bride standing in a cemetery.

156   INTERPRETING IMAGERY

What would you say is the artist's main idea in this picture? Is it *happiness* or is it *death?* You can choose details that support either main idea. And that is what is wrong with the picture. The image most people have of happiness has nothing to do with a cemetery. The image most people have of death has nothing to do with happiness.

If the artist had wanted to paint a picture that had only one main idea or one effect, all the details should have supported that idea. Suppose the artist had wanted you to feel the happiness of a young bride. Any number of details could have been chosen to show that feeling—but not the grave markers and ugly old trees of a cemetery. Suppose, on the other hand, that the artist had wanted you to get a feeling of coldness and gloom. A cemetery would have been perfect in that case—but not a happy bride.

Writers also use details to give a reader an image of a certain feeling. Read the paragraph below. Pay careful attention to the details described, and see if you can tell how the writer feels.

```
1        As I walked into the park, the sun was just setting, giving
2    the sky a warm, red glow. A pair of pigeons softly cooing at
3    each other were the only things to disturb the silence of the
4    moment. I took a deep breath of the delicate scent of the freshly
5    cut grass. Then I lay down, letting the tiny blades of grass
6    tickle my bare arms. As the sweet candy in my mouth slowly
7    melted, I thought how much like that candy this day had been.
```

The five sentences of the paragraph give you details about each of the five senses:

Sight — the warm, red glow of sunset
Sound — pigeons softly cooing
Smell — delicate scent of freshly cut grass
Touch — tiny blades of grass tickling the writer's arms
Taste — sweet candy melting in the writer's mouth

All of these details are pleasant to the senses. If all the things a person sees, hears, smells, feels, and tastes are pleasant, how must that person feel? All of these details paint an image of a person who is lighthearted, carefree, and happy with the world. A person in a different mood might sense this same scene in a very different way:

```
1        As I walked into the park, the sun was just setting, turning
2    the sky blood red. Two pigeons, the flying rats of the city, chat-
3    tered noisily, ruining any hope I might have had for a moment
```

4   of peace and quiet. The sick-sweet smell of freshly cut grass
5   made me sick to my stomach. As I lay down to rest, the tiny
6   blades of grass against my bare arms felt like a million tiny
7   needles jabbing at me. The sugary imitation cherry candy
8   melting in my mouth reminded me how cheap life had become.

The scene is exactly the same, but the way in which the details are sensed tells you something about the writer's mood.

Sight — blood red sky at sunset
Sound — noisy chattering of pigeons (flying rats)
Smell — sick-sweet smell of freshly cut grass
Touch — grass jabbing at the writer's arms like a million tiny needles
Taste — sugary imitation cherry candy

All of these details are unpleasant to the senses. If all the things a person sees, hears, smells, feels, and tastes are unpleasant, how must that person feel? All of these details paint an image of a person who is grouchy, out of sorts, and irritated by the world—exactly the opposite image created in the first paragraph.

The writer's mood is not directly stated in either paragraph. Yet the reader is able to get a feeling about the writer's mood from the physical details in the paragraphs. The writer has painted a picture, or created an image, of the real, physical scene. The reader gets a certain feeling about that image that makes it possible to make an inference about something unstated, in this case, the writer's mood.

IMAGE	IMAGE
(real, physical details)	*(unstated quality)*
pleasant sensations	good mood, lighthearted; carefree
unpleasant sensations	bad mood; grouchy; out of sorts

This use of real, physical details to make you understand something unstated is called **imagery**. Imagery, then, is a type of figurative language. There is a deeper meaning that can be inferred from the physical image the writer has painted with words.

In the following exercise, you will be able to make several inferences about a person in a story by paying attention to the images created by the supporting details.

Exercise A

DIRECTIONS: Read the following story, paying careful attention to the sights, sounds, feelings, smells, and tastes the writer describes. Then, answer the questions that follow the story by circling the letter of the best answer. Answers and explanations are given in the Answer Key at the end of the unit.

1   There is a place in this city that will always be my own. It is
2   a tiny park, a park most people don't even notice. At the heart of
3   the park is a broken fountain. People have scratched their
4   names on its sides. Some of the names have begun to disappear
5   with the passing of time. Others are scratched so deeply that
6   the fountain will always carry the scars of the meetings with
7   the people who carved them.
8   Last night, I walked to the park to visit my fountain. The
9   cold light of the moon showed all its present defects and gave
10 no hint of its former beauty. The hollow sound of a distant
11 church bell warned me that it was too late for my visit. But I
12 was tired, and I had come so far to be near my only friend.
13   As I sat down on the edge of my fountain, the coldness of
14 the lifeless stone sent shivers through my body. But still I
15 stayed, unable to move. I took the last stale cigarette from my
16 pack and choked on its thick, dry smoke. I thought how much
17 like my life that cigarette was. It was something I couldn't give
18 up, yet something I did not really want. My fountain under-
19 stands what it is like to be so close to death yet still alive.

1. The image in the story with which the speaker most closely identifies is
   (A) a lifeless stone
   (B) a stale cigarette
   (C) a broken fountain
   (D) a distant church bell
   (E) the cold light of the moon

2. From the way the speaker describes the scene, you can infer that the speaker feels
   (A) broken-hearted
   (B) sleepy
   (C) sick
   (D) cheerful
   (E) depressed

3. The names scratched on the sides of the fountain probably represent the fact that, in the speaker's own life,
   (A) no one has really cared about him
   (B) everyone has tried to hurt him
   (C) some people have hurt him deeply and some have only hurt him a little
   (D) some people have affected him deeply while others are nearly forgotten
   (E) everyone has left him, and he has forgotten them all

4. The writer chose to have the fountain appear in moonlight rather than in sunlight. This is probably because moonlight creates an image of
   (A) madness
   (B) gloom
   (C) peace
   (D) ugliness
   (E) poor eyesight

5. The only sound in the story is the sound of a distant church bell. The most likely reason that the speaker describes the sound as *hollow* (line 10) is that
   (A) the speaker is not a religious person
   (B) the speaker is hard of hearing
   (C) the speaker thinks of everything in his life as empty and meaningless
   (D) the speaker finds unhappiness in everything he sees and hears
   (E) the speaker doesn't want to be reminded of how late it is

So far in this unit, all the writers have used imagery that involves the five physical senses. In other words, the way a person sees, hears, feels, smells, and tastes the world about him has told you something about that person. In the last exercise, you read about a person who called a broken fountain "my only friend"—which told you something about that person. In the following exercise, the writer describes two people by describing something they own. This, too, is a kind of imagery.

Exercise B

DIRECTIONS: Read the following three paragraphs. After the paragraphs, you will find a list of descriptive words and phrases. Place a **J** for Jay in the blanks next to the words and phrases that would most likely be true of Jay. Place an **M** for Marty in the blanks next to the words and phrases that would most likely be true of Marty.

1 My friends Jay and Marty are as different as two people
2 can be. For example, both of them bought new cars last year.
3 But their choices were as different as they are.
4 Jay found a 1955 Packard Caribbean, a car I had never
5 heard of before. Leave it to Jay to find something like that car!
6 The body of the car is painted black near the bottom and white
7 on the hood, trunk, and just under the windows. In between the
8 black and the white, there is a wide stripe of hot pink that runs
9 the entire 18 feet of the car. The stripes of color are separated by
10 strips of dazzling chrome. The hot pink vinyl seats and convert-
11 ible top could really hurt your eyes on a sunny day. Of course,
12 the top is up only when it rains. When I went for a ride in Jay's
13 car, I noticed an odd-looking shiny black box fastened to the
14 back seat just behind the driver. Knowing Jay, I should have
15 guessed what it was, but I asked anyway. Jay turned around,
16 flipped up the lid, and there it was—a bar, complete with a
17 small ice chest!
18 Marty's car is a completely different story. He bought a
19 solid black 1974 Volkswagen. He is proud that he gets more
20 miles per gallon with his car than Jay gets with his 275 horse-
21 power V-8 engine. Marty particularly liked the fact that his VW
22 has no fancy options. It doesn't even have a radio. Marty
23 explains that he only needs a car to get from one place to
24 another. He just doesn't see any sense in spending a lot of
25 money on a flashy car.

____ 1. practical

____ 2. has an odd sense of humor

____ 3. likes flashy clothes

____ 4. is careful of how he spends money

____ 5. out for a good time

____ 6. no-nonsense type

INTERPRETING IMAGERY

As you learned in the last unit, writers often use figurative language to help them describe a feeling or an idea. The writer draws on your feelings about the usual meanings of words to understand those same words used in a figurative sense. For example, when a writer says that "Mac is a pig," you must use your understanding of the word *pig* to understand something about Mac. Imagery can work in this same way. A writer may use figurative language, such as a simile or a metaphor, to give you a certain image. In the following exercise, the writer builds a metaphor that asks you to get an image of a sailing ship. Using this image, you can then understand what the writer is trying to say about something entirely different—marriage.

Exercise C

DIRECTIONS: Read the following three paragraphs and then answer the questions that follow by circling the letter of the best answer. Answers and explanations are given in the Answer Key at the end of the unit.

1 The great ship of marriage sails an uneven course. In calm
2 waters, her captain and her mate have no trouble keeping her
3 on course. But storms come in the lives of every ship. Though
4 some captains bravely try to weather the storm, others are
5 quick to cry "Abandon ship" when the going gets rough.
6   Like marriage, a ship is only as good as the stuff of which it
7 is made. It also takes time to build a good ship. A ship hastily
8 made of cheap wood and held together by glue will sail a short
9 way before it sinks. A ship built slowly and carefully of steel
10 will weather many storms. Only a major disaster will shorten
11 the life of such a ship.
12   On some ships, there is only one captain. The mate is there
13 only to carry out the captain's orders. On these ships, there is
14 always the danger of rebellion or mutiny. On other ships, the
15 captain and the mate share the job of keeping the ship in shape
16 and on course. On these ships, the sailing is not always smooth,
17 but at least the crew works together for the good of both the ship
18 and themselves.

1. When the writer points out the difference between sailing in calm water and sailing in a storm, he is making a statement about the fact that a marriage
   (A) is usually happier in good weather
   (B) can last only if both people can keep their tempers
   (C) is easier to maintain in good times
   (D) can't last through hard times
   (E) always ends when hard times hit

2. Captains who are quick to cry "Abandon ship" (lines 4-5) are like people who
   (A) run away from responsibility
   (B) are never home when they're needed
   (C) hide whenever there is trouble
   (D) ask for a divorce after the first big fight
   (E) are weak when they should be strong

3. If two people get married after knowing each other for only a few days, to what would the author compare their marriage?
   (A) a ship on the brink of a major disaster
   (B) a hastily made wooden ship
   (C) a ship with only one captain
   (D) a ship in a storm
   (E) a carefully built steel ship

4. In a marriage in which both husband and wife work and both share the household chores, there is
   (A) a crew that works together for the good of the ship
   (B) always the danger of rebellion or mutiny
   (C) only one captain
   (D) always smooth sailing
   (E) a major disaster coming

ANSWER KEY—UNIT XII

Exercise A

1. (C) a broken fountain

   Answers (A), (D), and (E) are all details the speaker talks about, but they are not things to which the speaker feels close or with which the speaker identifies. Although the speaker states that, *"I thought how much like my life that cigarette was,"* it is the fountain that would understand what the speaker means by that statement. The fountain would understand because the speaker feels in many ways like that fountain—close to death yet still alive.

2. (E) depressed

   All of the images in the story are gloomy and depressing, which suggests that the speaker is also depressed.

3. (D) some people have affected him deeply while others are nearly forgotten.

   The speaker first states that some *"names have begun to disappear with the passing of time."* In other words, as time goes on, the memory of some people in a person's life fade away. But there are other names that have made a deeper impression, deep enough that *"the fountain will always carry the scars of the meetings with the people who carved them."* The reader must translate this image to what happens in a person's life. Some people create such a deep impression, affect one's life so deeply, that they will be remembered to the end of one's life.

   There is nothing in the story to support the idea that no one has ever really cared about the speaker (answer A); all we know is that there doesn't seem to be anyone at the moment. Answers (B) and (C) mention hurt, something that might be suggested by the use of the word *scars*. However, there is nothing in the rest of the story to support this interpretation. The speaker doesn't seem to be hurt, only tired of living. The interpretation given in answer (D) is more in keeping with the tone of the rest of the story. Answer (E) does not take into account the meaning of always bearing the scars of the meetings with some people.

164 INTERPRETING IMAGERY

4. (B) gloom

   This is the only one of the five answer choices that reflects the tone of the story. Since the moonlight shows all the fountain's *"present defects and none of its former beauty"* (lines 9-10), at least to the eye of the speaker, the reader gets a sense of the speaker's gloom and depression.

5. (C) the speaker thinks of everything in his life as empty and meaningless

   The word *hollow* means "being empty on the inside." The use of the word to describe the sound of the church bell suggests that the speaker finds the world about him empty, and hence meaningless. This idea can also be found in the last lines of the story in which the speaker finds his life so empty and meaningless that he feels close to death.

Exercise B

M	1.	practical
J	2.	has an odd sense of humor
J	3.	likes flashy clothes
M	4.	is careful of how he spends money
J	5.	out for a good time
M	6.	no-nonsense type

The fact that Jay chose a car with such wild colors and has even installed a bar in the back seat would suggest that 2, 3, and 5 are true of him. The fact that Marty chose a car that was practical and economical suggests that 1, 4, and 6 are true of him.

Exercise C

1. **(C) is easier to maintain in good times**

   The reader must substitute marriage for the ship. A ship sailing in good and bad weather is like a marriage in good and bad times. In bad times, some people abandon their marriages.

2. **(D) ask for a divorce after the first big fight**

   The idea of abandoning a ship equals the idea of abandoning a marriage. The only choice that suggests abandoning a marriage is the one that mentions divorce, the total break-up of the marriage.

3. **(B) a hastily made wooden ship**

   The sense of the second paragraph is that a good marriage is one that is built over a period of time, one with a solid foundation. The writer then talks about the two different types of ships (marriages)—ones that are built too quickly and out of bad materials and ones that are built slowly and carefully out of strong material. A hasty marriage, like the one described in the question, is most likely the hastily built ship.

4. **(A) a crew that works together for the good of the ship**

   The situation described in the question is like the situation described in lines 14–18.

UNIT XIII: READING POETRY

As you have discovered in the last two units, writers use figurative language to give you a clearer idea of what they think or how they feel. As a reader, you go beyond the simple or dictionary meaning of the words to draw some conclusion about the writer's message.

Figurative language is used in the same way in poetry. In fact, almost every poem you read will use figurative language to take you beyond the simple meanings of words.

Poets, or writers of poetry, spend a lot of time choosing the words they will use. The words must give the reader exactly the feeling and the meaning that the poet wants the reader to understand. Even the sound of the word is important. For this reason, as a reader, you will find that you must spend a little more time reading. You will have to pay attention to the sounds of the words and the figurative meaning that comes through the words. For example, study the word below:

frozen

sound

simple meaning

figurative meaning

First, think about the sound of the word. There are many words that mean the same thing as *frozen;* why should a poet choose this word? How do you feel when you hear the word or say the word slowly? What is the difference between saying *"I'm cold"* and saying *"I'm frozen"*? Is there a difference in the feeling you get from the sound of the word?

Now, think about the simple dictionary definition of the word. What does it mean? If something is frozen, it is extremely cold; it is solid; it does not move; it is lifeless.

Put the feeling you get from the sound of the word together with the simple dictionary meaning of the word. What special or figurative meaning does the word suggest? What other words give you the same feeling? Think of something that is frozen—for example, an ice cube. What feelings do you get from the mental picture of an ice cube? Now, imagine that you are trapped in a giant ice cube. How do you feel? Can you move? Can you feel anything?

Words do not stand alone in poetry. You must use all your feelings about the individual words and apply them to the lines of poetry in which they are used. Look at the two lines below and think about what the word *frozen* suggests.

> Life is a barren field
> Frozen with snow.

Now, try to answer the questions below.

1. The poet is talking about
   (A) the mountains
   (B) a field covered with snow
   (C) man's life
   (D) an island

2. The word *frozen* in the line of poetry above most nearly means
   (A) heavy
   (B) empty
   (C) cold
   (D) dead

Can you answer these two questions without reading more of the poem?

The first question asks you to find out what the poet is talking about. Did you recognize the type of figurative language the poet is using? It is a metaphor. The poet compares life to a barren field frozen with snow. Therefore, the correct answer to the first question is (C).

But what does this mean? How is a person's life like a barren field frozen with snow? Do you know what the word *barren* means? If you don't know that it means *bare* or *without life,* does the sound of the word suggest its meaning? Even if you aren't sure how the word is pronounced or what its exact meaning is, the line gives you good clues. Think for a moment about the image of a field that is frozen and covered with snow. Which of the answer choices to the second question best describes this image? Is it heavy? Is it empty? Is it cold? Is it dead? Think back to the image of yourself, a human life, trapped inside a giant ice cube. Which of the answer choices best describes how you feel? Doesn't a frozen life suggest nothingness, a kind of death?

All of the words the poet uses in this metaphor suggest death. If a field is barren, there is no life, nothing on the field. If the field is frozen, whatever life there might have been would have been killed. If the field is covered with snow, all the life would be covered up and trapped underneath the snow. Therefore, in these lines of poetry, the word *frozen* most nearly means *dead* (answer choice D).

Why would a poet compare life to a feeling of death? To answer this question you will have to read more of the poem.

> Hold fast to dreams
> For when dreams go
> Life is a barren field
> Frozen with snow.

The two new lines you have just read tell you *when* life can be compared to a barren field frozen with snow. When dreams go, when a person no longer hopes or dreams, that person's life becomes a kind of death. His life is a barren field; it produces nothing. His life is frozen; he doesn't move, or change, or grow. His life is trapped just like the life of grass is trapped under a field of snow. For this reason, the poet tells you to hold fast to (hold onto) your dreams.

In order to draw these conclusions about the poet's message, you had to pay careful attention to the words the poet used. The poet depends on the reader's feelings about the sounds of the words and about the meanings of the words to unlock the figurative meaning of the poem.

Now, read the entire poem and see how the sounds of some words as well as the feelings you have about the words themselves help you draw a conclusion about the poet's message.

> Hold fast to dreams
> For if dreams die
> Life is a broken-winged bird
> That cannot fly.
>
> Hold fast to dreams
> For when dreams go
> Life is a barren field
> Frozen with snow.
>
> Langston Hughes

How do the first four lines of the poem fit into the figurative meaning you found in the last four lines? What does the metaphor in the third and fourth lines suggest? What mental picture do you have of a bird? Do you think of a free spirit flying to great heights? What happens to that image of a bird if its wings are broken?

Once again, you must think of words with their usual meanings to get the figurative meaning of the lines of poetry. If you cannot draw a conclusion about the poet's message from the words in one line, the lines that come before and after that line will help you find out what the poet is talking about. The words in the poem do not stand alone; they work together as figurative language, the language of poetry, a language that says more and says it with power.

Langston Hughes, the poet who wrote the poem you have been studying, took his experience as a Black man living in America, wrapped it up in figurative language, and gave it to the world. He chose his words carefully, knowing that readers would take their own experiences and feelings about those words and use them to feel as he felt. By using figurative language, Hughes is able to draw a clear and powerful picture of how he felt and what he wants the reader to understand.

Exercise A

DIRECTIONS: Read the poem below. It is about the city of Chicago, Illinois. Then answer the questions that follow the poem. If you aren't sure about the answers, you may want to reread Unit XI. Check your answers in the Answer Key at the end of the unit.

Chicago

Hog Butcher for the World,
Tool maker, Stacker of Wheat,
Player with Railroads and the Nation's Freight Handler;
Stormy, husky, brawling,
City of the Big Shoulders . . .

Carl Sandburg

1. A good example of the type of *figurative language* known as *personification* is
   (A) Tool maker
   (B) Nation's Freight Handler
   (C) City of the Big Shoulders

2. The words that give you the feeling of a city struggling to be powerful are
   (A) Stormy, husky, brawling
   (B) Tool maker
   (C) Stacker of Wheat

3. When the author uses the phrase "Hog Butcher for the World," he means that Chicago is
   (A) a great place to raise pigs
   (B) the city with the biggest butcher shop
   (C) a major supplier of meat

ANSWER KEY—UNIT XIII

1. (C) City of Big Shoulders

   Cities do not have shoulders. The poet is speaking of a city as he would of a person. Big shoulders on a person might mean that that person is strong. The poet wants the reader to feel that Chicago is a big, strong city. This use of figurative language, writing about a nonliving thing as though it were a person, is called personification.

2. (A) Stormy, husky, brawling

   The words *stormy, husky,* and *brawling* give the reader a feeling of the fight for power. Even if you are not sure of the exact meanings of the words as they are used in the poem, the sound of the words should give you a feeling of power, of a city that is determined to be the best.

3. (C) a major supplier of meat

   When this poem was written, Chicago had the largest stockyards in the world. From Chicago, meat was sent all over the country, and some of this meat was then shipped to other countries. Even if you did not know this fact, you can tell from the other lines of the poem that the poet is talking about the kinds of industry that are in Chicago. Neither answer (A) nor answer (B) fit with the figurative meaning of the whole poem.

UNIT XIV: VOCABULARY SKILLS—
RECOGNIZING PREFIXES

Pearl often has dreams in which she sees things happen before they happen. She can <u>foresee</u> accidents before they happen. Being able to <u>foretell</u> the future is a gift for which Pearl is very grateful. She once told her husband not to take the 5:15 train home from work, the train he always took, because of a dream she had had. That same evening, the 5:15 was involved in a horrible wreck in which many people were badly hurt. Without Pearl's <u>foreknowledge</u> of the accident, her husband might have been one of the injured people.

Look at the underlined words in the paragraph above: *foresee; foretell; foreknowledge*. Each word begins with the same four letters—*fore*. Without the first four letters, you have three very common words:

    see
    tell
    knowledge

By adding *fore* in front of each of these common words, a new word with a new meaning has been formed:

    foresee = see something before it happens
    foretell = tell about something before it happens
    foreknowledge = knowledge about something before it happens

The new meanings still have something to do with the meanings of the original words. The original meaning has been changed to include the idea of *coming before*. The original word is the main word or **root** of the new word. The part that has been added in front of the root is a **prefix.**

Many words in English are made up of a prefix and a root. If you know the meaning of the root, and if you know the general meaning of the prefix, you will be able to understand the meaning of a word that is a combination of the two. For example, if you were told to read the *foreword* of a book, where would you find it?

        prefix   +   **root**
        fore   word

You know from what you have just learned that the prefix *fore* adds the meaning of *coming before* to the root. If you look in the front of the book *before* the first chapter, you will find the *foreword*. A foreword is something the writer adds in front of the main part of a book to tell you something about what you are going to read.

In the following pages, you will learn the meanings of some of the most common prefixes. By learning the meanings of these prefixes, you will be able to understand the meanings of words that use these prefixes. Let's look at the first group of prefixes:

re: means *again*

EXAMPLES: If I like a book I have just read, I often *reread* it.
Somehow I managed to live through my childhood, but I don't think I would like to *relive* it.

re: also means *back* or *backward*

EXAMPLES: When you *replace* the book on the shelf, make sure you place it in the same spot.
Because of a defect in the engine, all those cars are being *recalled*.

pre: means *before* or *earlier*

EXAMPLES: If you don't want Aunt Helen to pay the delivery charges, you can *prepay* the charges yourself.
There is no need to plan anything; we have *preplanned* the whole day for you.

post: means *after* or *later*

EXAMPLES: Since you don't have enough money in the bank to cover this check, you can *postdate* it, and we'll promise not to cash it until that date.
Some people claim that the economy is always better during a war. In *postwar* years, they claim, there are fewer jobs and more people looking for work.

VOCABULARY SKILLS—RECOGNIZING PREFIXES

In the following exercise, you will be able to get the meaning you want by adding a prefix to a common root.

Exercise A

DIRECTIONS: Fill in the blanks by adding either the prefix *re* or the prefix *pre* to the root word that follows the blank so that you get the meaning given in parentheses at the end of the sentence. Check your answers in the Answer Key at the end of the unit.

1. Before the movie started, we saw a ____view of the picture that would be playing next. (viewing part of a film *before* it is shown in the theater)

2. Let's buy this. It's ____cooked, and we won't have to do anything but heat it up. (already cooked before it was packaged)

3. I know you are busy, but could you ____arrange your schedule so that I can see you for a little while? (arrange your schedule *again* in a different way)

4. We'd be happy to order that sewing machine for you, but you must ____pay at least half the price today. (pay some money *in advance*)

5. Since I'm not driving tonight, I'll have a ____fill on my drink. (fill up *again*)

6. The letter I wrote to Jose was in my jeans and went through the washing machine. I guess I'll have to ____write it. (write it over *again*)

7. I was searching for my jacket. Since it was at the bottom of my suitcase, I made a mess. Now I'll have to ____pack. (pack *again*)

8. If you ____soak your work clothes for a few hours, they will be much easier to wash. (soak in a cleaning solution *before* you actually wash the clothes)

VOCABULARY SKILLS—RECOGNIZING PREFIXES

A word can be changed to have the opposite meaning by adding a negative prefix. Study the following nine prefixes, paying special attention to how they change the meanings of the root words in the examples.

un: means *not*

EXAMPLES: What may be very important to you may be *unimportant* to me.

You'll have to cook these eggs a little longer. I can't eat them this way—they're almost *uncooked*.

il: means *not*

EXAMPLES: Who told you that smoking marijuana is legal in California? As far as I know, it is still *illegal* in every state.

Far from being a logical conclusion, your statement is the most *illogical* thing I have heard in years.

im: means *not*

EXAMPLES: Although my father always told me that everything is possible, I have found through experience that some things are *impossible*.

I can't be patient and just wait for something to happen. I'm too *impatient;* I'd rather make things happen.

in: means *not*

EXAMPLES: I was told that you were capable of typing 80 words a minute, but you are *incapable* of typing 30 words a minute.

I want the complete story on the fire, but this newspaper story on it is *incomplete*. It doesn't even say whether the fire was put out.

ir: means *not*

    EXAMPLES: Even a regular day has some *irregular* event buried in it.

                       Teachers talk a great deal about having me read relevant books; yet, what they call *irrelevant* may be very important to my life.

non: means *not*

    EXAMPLES: It may seem like *nonsense* to you, but it makes perfect sense to me.

                       Nonsmokers claim to have a better sense of taste than smokers.

anti: means *against*

    EXAMPLES: Members of the *anticruelty* society want to see an end to cruelty to animals.

                       To protect your car when the temperature falls below freezing, you must use *antifreeze*.

dis: means *not* or *apart from*

    EXAMPLES: Joan wants me to approve of what she did, but I *disapprove* of anyone who lies—no matter what the reason.

                       You appeared out of nowhere; now you can *disappear*.

mis: means *wrong(ly); bad(ly);* or *lack of*

    EXAMPLES: My brother has all the good fortune; I seem to have nothing but *misfortune*.

                       We ask our children to behave; yet, when they *misbehave*, we must look at ourselves to see that they are not just following our example.

VOCABULARY SKILLS—RECOGNIZING PREFIXES

Although knowing the meanings of prefixes may give you the clue to the meanings of many English words, you must beware of words that only begin with the same letters as the prefix:

    unto   interpret
    illness   distress
    imitate   mission

None of these words is formed with a prefix. You will not be able to get the meanings of these words by using the meaning of the prefix. In the following exercise, you will be faced with a list of words, some of which are a combination of a prefix and a root and some of which have nothing to do with a prefix. Review the nine prefixes you studied on pages 176 and 177, and then do Exercise B.

Exercise B

DIRECTIONS: When the prefixes *un, il, im, in, ir, non, dis,* or *mis* are attached to a root, the meaning of the new word is the opposite of the meaning of the root word alone. Place a check mark next to each word in the following list that is a combination of one of these prefixes and a root word. Check your answers in the Answer Key at the end of the unit.

1. irresponsible ____
2. discuss ____
3. imperfect ____
4. unknown ____
5. nonunion ____
6. mistress ____
7. income ____
8. dishonest ____
9. illiterate ____
10. irrational ____
11. imagine ____
12. insane ____
13. nonfiction ____
14. understand ____
15. misread ____
16. illustrate ____
17. irritate ____
18. nonviolent ____
19. immoral ____
20. inhuman ____
21. disagree ____
22. unhappy ____
23. misunderstand ____
24. illegitimate ____

In the next exercise, you will be asked to choose a prefix and a root to get a word that has a certain meaning. You will need to put the meaning of a prefix together with the meaning of a root to get a word that has the meaning you want.

VOCABULARY SKILLS—RECOGNIZING PREFIXES

Exercise C

DIRECTIONS: Choose a prefix from the list of prefixes and a root from the list of roots to form a word that has the definition given. Write your answer in the blank next to the definition. Each prefix and each root will only be used once. Check your answers in the Answer Key at the end of the unit.

Prefix	Root
re	suppose
re	legible
pre	stop
post	place
un	play
il	test
im	finished
in	social
ir	proper
non	pay
anti	connect
dis	direct
mis	replaceable

1. _____ not legible (readable)

2. _____ not able to be replaced

3. _____ to break the connection between two wires

4. _____ to play over again

5. _____ without a stop

6. _____ to suppose beforehand

7. _____ to put in the wrong place

8. _____ to pay money back that is owed

9. _____ not proper

10. _____ a test given after a student has finished his studies

11. _____ not direct

12. _____ against being sociable

13. _____ not finished

Often, the same root word can be used with several different prefixes. In the following exercise, you will be given two words to choose from. Both words have the same root; only the prefixes are different. In order to choose the word with the correct meaning for the sentence, you will need to know what meaning the prefix gives to the root.

Exercise D

DIRECTIONS: Read the sentences below. Decide which of the two words under the sentence best fits the sentence. Write the correct answer in the blank provided. Check your answers in the Answer Key at the end of the unit.

1. I couldn't believe what I was reading the first time, so I had to _____ it.

    reread   misread

2. I didn't leave the egg in the water long enough, so the center is _____.

    precooked   uncooked

3. I've checked my letter over carefully so John won't find a _____.

    retake   mistake

4. Please check the newspaper for the weather _____ for tomorrow.

    miscast   forecast

5. My children came running through the kitchen with muddy feet just after I scrubbed the floor. Now I'll have to _____ it.

    unwash   rewash

6. The word "store" is _____ as "stone" in the book I'm reading.

        misprinted   reprinted

7. Long ago, the federal government passed _____ legislation to stop the growth of monopolies called trusts.

        antitrust   mistrust

8. Gail's chocolate cake tastes _____ anything you have ever eaten before.

        dislike   unlike

ANSWER KEY—UNIT XIV

Exercise A

1. preview; the prefix *pre* means *before* or *earlier*
2. precooked; the prefix *pre* means *before*
3. rearrange; the prefix *re* means *again*
4. prepay; the prefix *pre* means *beforehand*
5. refill; the prefix *re* means *again*
6. rewrite; the prefix *re* means *again*
7. repack; the prefix *re* means *again*
8. presoak; the prefix *pre* means *before*

Exercise B

You should have placed a check mark after each of the following:

1. irresponsible; it means *not* responsible
3. imperfect; it means *not* perfect
4. unknown; it means *not* known
5. nonunion; it means *not* union (or not a member of a union)
8. dishonest; it means *not* honest
9. illiterate; it means *not* literate *(literate* means *being able to read)*
10. irrational; it means *not* rational
12. insane; it means *not* sane
13. nonfiction; it means *not* fiction
15. misread; it means *not* read *correctly*
18. nonviolent; it means *not* violent
19. immoral; it means *not* moral
20. inhuman; it means *not* human
21. disagree; it means *not* agree
22. unhappy; it means *not* happy
23. misunderstand; it means *not* understand *correctly*
24. illegitimate; it means *not* legitimate

Note: Numbers 2, 6, 7, 11, 14, 16, and 17 are not a combination of a prefix and a root.

Exercise C

1. illegible
2. irreplaceable
3. disconnect
4. replay
5. nonstop
6. presuppose
7. misplace
8. repay
9. improper
10. posttest
11. indirect
12. antisocial
13. unfinished

Exercise D

1. reread; you need a word that means to read again (the prefix *re* means *again*)
2. uncooked; you need a word that means not cooked (the prefix *un* means *not*)
3. mistake; you need a word that means something that can be taken wrongly (the prefix *mis* means *wrongly*)
4. forecast; you need a word that means a report (or cast) before an expected event (the prefix *fore* means *coming before*)
5. rewash; you need a word that means wash again (the prefix *re* means *again*)
6. misprinted; you need a word that means incorrectly printed (the prefix *mis* means *incorrectly* or *wrongly*)
7. antitrust; you need a word that means against trusts (the prefix *anti* means *against*)
8. unlike; you need a word that means not like (the prefix *un* means *not*)

READING SKILLS REVIEW

DIRECTIONS: Read the following five selections. After each selection, there are a few questions. The questions will give you a chance to review the skills you have learned in this book. Answer each question based on the information in the selection by circling the letter of the **best** answer.

The definitions of the **Words You Need to Know**, which are listed before every selection, can be found in the **Dictionary** at the back of the book.

1

Words You Need To Know

obese   retain
capable   muttered
ashamed   interview

1   Cora had tried for years to take off a few pounds. Did I say a
2   few pounds? Well, I can tell you she needed to do a lot more than
3   that. Cora was my best friend, and although I loved her dearly,
4   I was actually ashamed to go out with her. She weighed over
5   two hundred pounds and was only about five feet, five inches
6   tall. Day after weary day I nagged, I pleaded, I yelled. Nothing.
7   My efforts did absolutely nothing to get Cora moving toward
8   having a nicer figure.
9   Cora was having trouble getting a job. I figured that people
10 just didn't like her looks. She was a good typist and could even
11 take shorthand. She had a good telephone voice and the ability
12 to make decisions quickly. But how was anyone going to know
13 that if she was never given a chance?
14 One day Cora went for an interview for a job as a secre-
15 tary. The job was only for eight weeks, and the salary was low,
16 but it was better than nothing. Besides, it was a chance for Cora
17 to get some experience and another job reference; although the
18 one job reference she had didn't seem to help her get other jobs.

19 Cora started her new job on June twenty-seventh. Her boss,
20 Mrs. Hogan, was a very pleasant but businesslike type. Cora
21 told me all about her that first day after work.
22 "Oh, Mrs. Hogan is really great. She spent a lot of time
23 explaining the responsibilities of the job to me. And, she invited
24 me to her house for dinner next Friday night."
25 After work on Friday, Cora rushed home to put on her
26 latest purchase. It was a tentlike dress, which was about the
27 only thing that would fit her that week.
28 Sitting across from Mrs. Hogan at dinner that evening,
29 Cora ate as little as possible, not wanting to stuff herself in
30 front of her employer.
31 "Cora, you eat so little. I'm surprised that you retain
32 weight."
33 Embarrassed, Cora looked across at her new boss. "I guess
34 I eat a lot more than this when I'm home. It's no fun living
35 alone. I guess I eat just to make the time go by."
36 "Cora, I like you." Mrs. Hogan smiled across the table and
37 continued. "In the short time we've worked together I've seen
38 how capable you are, and I'd like to help you if you'll let me."
39 Two tiny tears ran down Cora's cheeks, and she brushed
40 them away with her sleeve. "How can you help?" she muttered.
41 "Even my best friend has been yelling and nagging at me to
42 lose weight. How can you know how I feel? You're slim. You
43 could never know how it feels to be fat and have people make
44 fun of you behind your back." Cora sat quietly with her head
45 down.
46 "Cora, look at me." Mrs. Hogan's voice had a sharp, no-
47 nonsense ring to it as she spoke. "Listen, and look." She handed
48 Cora a picture of an obese woman who stood in front of a
49 house. The woman's form almost completely blocked the build-
50 ing. "That's me, Cora. That was taken seven years ago when I
51 weighed more than you do this very minute."
52 Cora sighed. She hoped that this woman, who had ob-
53 viously solved her own weight problem, would be able to help
54 her.

1. The best title for the story is
   (A) Slim at Last
   (B) You Can If I Can
   (C) Mirrors Don't Lie
   (D) Nag a Little More
   (E) Looking for a Job

2. Based on the information in the passage, the reader can conclude that
   (A) Cora will spend many years at this job
   (B) Cora doesn't have enough skills for an office job
   (C) Cora has been overweight for most of her life
   (D) Cora's best friend didn't care enough about her to help
   (E) Cora had a whole closet full of tentlike dresses

3. When Cora went to Mrs. Hogan's house for dinner, she
   (A) stuffed herself
   (B) didn't eat at all
   (C) ate very little
   (D) asked for seconds
   (E) ate what Mrs. Hogan ate

4. The words "job reference" (line 17) most nearly mean
   (A) a report on previous job performance
   (B) progress on the job
   (C) on-the-job training
   (D) a way to collect unemployment
   (E) a chance to get a new job

5. When the author says "get Cora moving toward having a nicer figure. . . . ," she means to get Cora to
   (A) a store to buy tight-fitting clothes
   (B) work harder on exercises
   (C) work on improving her math skills
   (D) move to a different town
   (E) work on losing weight

2

Words You Need to Know

census	supervision
trend	effectiveness
regularly	convenience

1 The first U.S. census was taken in 1790. At that time, there
2 was an average of 5.7 people in a family in America. The 1900
3 census showed an average of 4.6 people per family. By 1950, the
4 average size of an American family had dropped to 3.5 people.
5 This trend toward smaller families has continued to the present
6 day.
7 There is no ideal number of children for a person to have.
8 Whether and when to have children is a choice that each person
9 must make. The census figures show that more and more people
10 are choosing not to have children. They can make this choice
11 more easily now because of the many modern methods of birth
12 control.
13 There is no one method of birth control that is perfect for
14 everybody. Choosing a method of birth control is just as
15 personal as deciding whether or not to have children. For
16 example, certain religions do not permit some of the methods of
17 birth control.
18 People can choose any one of a number of methods that
19 work well and that aren't costly. None is 100% certain, and no
20 method will work if it is not used properly. A person will get the
21 best results by choosing a method that will be used *regularly*.
22 A person who wants to practice birth control should
23 compare all of the different methods. The best method for each
24 person can be chosen with the help of a doctor. The Planned
25 Parenthood center, local health department, or hospital family
26 planning center can also help.
27 Some methods require a doctor's supervision. These
28 methods can work better than the methods that can be found on
29 a drugstore shelf. For example, no one can get the birth control
30 pill without a doctor's okay. The pill is not for everyone. It
31 should be used only upon a doctor's advice.

A method that one person likes may not be liked by another. How, then, can a person decide which method to use? There are several things to think about before choosing a method of birth control:

Safety — The ideal method of birth control must be safe to use. A doctor can tell the person whether a method is safe.

Effectiveness — Will the method do what it's supposed to? Will it work? While any method is better than none, not all are equally effective. And, too, a method can work well only if it is used properly and regularly.

Effect on Health — Women who have certain health problems cannot use some methods. A doctor can tell her which methods she cannot use. Too, some methods may cause a health problem for some women. If a woman finds that the method she is using causes discomfort, she should see a doctor. The discomfort may be the first sign of a health problem.

Convenience — The less a method gets in the way of a person's normal life, the better it is.

Cost — Many methods cannot really be called costly, though some cost a little more than others. If budget is a problem, a person can get advice from a clinic or Planned Parenthood center.

Personal Feelings — Personal feelings should be discussed with a doctor. Any method that is unpleasant for some reason is not likely to be used.

Although there are many methods of birth control from which to choose, there are just as many ways to find out about them. Today, anyone who wants to have a small family can.

Lines 32-57 adapted from *Contraception* (also published in Spanish as *Contracepcion*), published by the Planned Parenthood Association/Chicago Area (55 East Jackson Boulevard, Chicago, Illinois 60604). Reprinted by permission.

6. According to the information in the selection, which of the following is the most likely cause of the smaller size of American families?
   (A) Most people don't want children.
   (B) Certain religions don't permit large families.
   (C) There are so many methods of birth control people can use.
   (D) People now realize that there is no ideal number of children to have.
   (E) Doctors are telling people not to have children.

7. Which of the following is *not* a factor in choosing a method of birth control?
   (A) a person's religion
   (B) a person's budget
   (C) a person's health
   (D) a person's own feelings
   (E) a person's family size

8. According to the selection, some methods of birth control
   (A) are always dangerous
   (B) can cause health problems for some women
   (C) are 100% certain
   (D) can be used by anyone
   (E) should never be used

9. In the author's opinion, if you want to practice birth control, the *first* thing you should do is
   (A) ask your friends what methods they use
   (B) try all the methods until you find one you like
   (C) try one of the methods you can get at the drugstore
   (D) talk to your doctor and follow his advice
   (E) get a prescription for the pill

10. The reason the author mentions personal feelings as one thing to think about before choosing a method of birth control is probably because
    (A) a person must like the method well enough to use it regularly
    (B) some methods of birth control cause hurt feelings
    (C) some methods of birth control cause people to lose the sense of touch
    (D) birth control is a very personal matter
    (E) some methods of birth control are generally unpleasant

11. The reason the birth control pill should be used under a doctor's supervision is probably because
    (A) it causes health problems
    (B) it can lead to drug addiction
    (C) you can't get it without a prescription
    (D) it may cause health problems
    (E) doctors make a profit on it

3

Words You Need to Know

bowed   autumn
weariness

Troubled Woman

1 She stands
2 In the quiet darkness,
3 This troubled woman
4 Bowed by
5 Weariness and pain
6 Like an
7 Autumn flower
8 In the frozen rain,
9 Like a
10 Wind-blown autumn flower
11 That never lifts its head
12 Again

Langston Hughes

12. The word *bowed* most nearly means
    (A) dangerous
    (B) annoyed
    (C) burdened
    (D) angry
    (E) hurt

13. The main idea of this poem is that the woman's life seems
    (A) empty
    (B) hopeless
    (C) dull
    (D) lonely
    (E) dangerous

14. The poem includes a simile in which the author compares the woman to
    (A) the quiet darkness
    (B) weariness and pain
    (C) frozen rain
    (D) an autumn flower
    (E) trouble

15. Although people would not ordinarily use the word *autumn* to describe a flower (line 7), it helps the reader to picture
    (A) something colorful
    (B) something dead
    (C) something cold
    (D) something that is dying
    (E) something artificial

4

Words You Need to Know

poised	customer
uniform	quizzical
enormous	mumbled

1 Sometimes, even when I'm sure that I'm completely
2 normal, I become invisible. For example, yesterday I went to a
3 restaurant, looked around, and spotted an empty table in back.
4 I took my coat off and slid into the booth. There were at least
5 three other booths that were unoccupied. Glancing around, I
6 could see that there were only about seven other customers in
7 the whole place. A second look and I was now aware that four
8 people in gray and white uniforms stood ready and eager to

9 serve the hundreds of hungry and thirsty customers who
10 might make their way through the swinging doors.
11   The waiters and waitresses seemed prepared to take on an
12 army if necessary. As they went about their rounds, they were
13 able to wait on anyone and everyone—that is, everyone but me.
14 They looked over my head, through my body, and made a com-
15 plete circle around my booth. Not once did anyone seem to see
16 me! I silently pleaded, I smiled, I begged with my eyes, but it did
17 no good. Customers to the left and right of me were served.
18   For fifteen minutes I waited and hoped and finally cast up
19 a silent prayer or two that I, too, might be among the noticed.
20 Ah, at last my waitress.
21   She moved toward me and mumbled, "Are you all through?
22 Would you like anything else?"
23   I had all I could do to swallow and whisper in return,
24 "Those dishes aren't mine. I haven't been waited on yet." By
25 this time I was ready to scream.
26   The blank stare on the waitress's face turned slowly into
27 what she must have meant to be a sweet smile. "Oh, I'm sorry,"
28 she said. "I didn't even see you. I hadn't noticed you were
29 waiting." She really didn't have to point out the fact that,
30 despite my being 30 years old, five feet, six inches tall, and
31 weighing in at a rough 134 pounds, I was invisible. She con-
32 tinued to clear off dirty dishes and wiped the table with a dirty
33 rag, dumping crumbs onto my lap. "Can I take your order now,
34 Ma'am? What would you like?" She stood poised with booklet
35 and pen in hand.
36   I pulled myself upright on the bench and looked up at the
37 waitress. "Since I have been invisible to you for the last fifteen
38 minutes, I can't imagine why you think I want to eat here.
39 Invisible people eat invisible food, you know. So, thank you
40 anyway, there is nothing on your menu for me." I got up and
41 walked out, hungry but satisfied that I had said something and
42 made myself visible at last.

16. When the speaker went into the restaurant, the *first* thing she did was
    (A) take off her coat
    (B) slide into a booth
    (C) see the empty tables
    (D) talk with the waitress
    (E) look around for a seat

17. When the speaker used the phrase, "prepared to take on an army" (lines 12-13), she meant the waiters and waitresses were
    (A) going to enlist
    (B) ready to serve food
    (C) cooking typical army food
    (D) having a fight
    (E) prepared for a large group

18. The best title for the story is
    (A) The Invisible Woman
    (B) Dining Out
    (C) When Do We Eat?
    (D) Customer Service
    (E) A Fifteen-Minute Wait

19. The waitress probably didn't wait on the woman in the story because
    (A) She didn't like the way she looked
    (B) She had too many other customers
    (C) She wasn't paying attention to her work
    (D) she hated her job
    (E) she wasn't wearing her glasses

20. When the waitress finally came to take the order, the speaker
    (A) got up and left
    (B) wasn't ready
    (C) started crying
    (D) yelled at her
    (E) told her to forget it and left

5

Words You Need to Know

abilities	dependents
applicant	discriminate
limitations	director

---

1   When a person applies for a job, he or she is usually asked
2 to fill out a form. The form is an application for employment.
3 On most forms, the person will be asked to name the job he is

seeking. By stating the kind of job the person wants, the employer knows what the person feels he can do. The employer can also tell that person whether he has any jobs open that suit the person's interests and abilities.

An application form will ask a number of questions that the employer feels he needs to ask. First, the form will ask for the job seeker's name, address, and telephone number. If the employer decides to offer a job, he must know how to contact the person. Anyone who applies for work must also have a social security number. If the person doesn't already have one, he should apply for one before he starts to work. In this case, the applicant should write "number applied for" in the blank that asks for the social security number. For a number of reasons, employers include questions on their forms that ask about number of children (dependents), ownership or rental of a home, car ownership, military service, physical limitations, and marital status. It is against the law for employers to use this information to discriminate on the basis of a person's race, creed, color, national origin, sex, age, or religion.

The most important part of an application for employment is the Employment Record or Job History. This part must be filled in honestly and completely. A person's job history is important for two reasons. First, it will tell an employer what skills a person already has. If a future employer knows the names and addresses of past employers, he can call or write them to find out how good the person was at his job. The second reason that this section of the form is so important is that employers can find out how long a person has stayed on other jobs. If all past jobs lasted for several years, generally the employer concludes that the person will probably stay for a while if he takes a job offer. If all past jobs only lasted for a few months, and the reasons for leaving are not very good, the employer will probably not risk hiring that person. If there are gaps in the employment record that are not explained, the employer will probably assume the worst. For this reason, the applicant should explain any periods of time during which he was not employed.

On pages 197 and 198, you will find an application for employment. Read the following paragraphs about Judy Black and fill out the form just as Judy should.

Judy Black rents an apartment at 32 Vista Road in Elmwood, Florida. Her telephone number is 272-5515. On June 28, 1976, her divorce from her husband became final. Since she has three children (ages 4, 6, and 7), it is important that she find a job immediately. Because her ex-husband didn't want Judy to work, she has only held one job in her life. In September of 1974, she started work as a volunteer nurse's aide at City General Hospital Although City General likes her work, they do not have the funds to give her a paying job. Since she is not paid for her work at City General, Judy does not have a social security number. She applied for a number on June 29, the day before she applied for a job at the Elmwood Center for Handicapped Children.

Judy left Miller High School in Elmwood in June of 1967 after completing the 10th grade. She got married in July of that same year. On her honeymoon trip, she was involved in an auto accident that left her with a slight limp. The limp doesn't limit her activities. She has never been convicted of a crime, and she hasn't served in the armed forces.

Judy has heard that the Elmwood Center's day-care program for physically handicapped children needs nurse's aides. Because she is only 5'1" tall and weighs only 102 pounds, the director of the center told Judy that the work might be difficult for her since the job required some heavy lifting. Judy didn't feel that her height or weight had anything to do with her ability to work with the children. She asked to be allowed to fill out an application for employment, and she was given the form that appears on the following two pages.

ELMWOOD CENTER FOR HANDICAPPED CHILDREN

139 Chandler Street

Elmwood, Florida

DATE _____

NAME _____ PHONE _____

ADDRESS _____

POSITION APPLIED FOR _____

PERSONAL INFORMATION

SOCIAL SECURITY
NUMBER _____ SINGLE _____ MARRIED _____ OTHER _____

HEIGHT _____ WEIGHT _____ NUMBER OF DEPENDENTS _____ AGES OF DEPENDENTS _____

DO YOU HAVE ANY PHYSICAL LIMITATIONS?   YES ____   NO ____   (If yes, please specify)

_____

HAVE YOU BEEN CONVICTED OF A CRIME WITHIN THE PAST TEN YEARS?   YES ____   NO ____
(If yes, please furnish details, as dates, places, offenses, and penalties)

_____

CIRCLE HIGHEST GRADE COMPLETED IN SCHOOL   1 2 3 4 5 6 7 8 9 10 11 12 13 14 15 16

NAME OF SCHOOL LAST ATTENDED _____ DID YOU GRADUATE? ____

ADDRESS OF SCHOOL _____

HAVE YOU SERVED IN THE ARMED FORCES?   YES ____   NO ____
(If yes, give dates, rank attained, decorations, etc.)

_____

EMPLOYMENT RECORD

Employer and Address	Dates	Job Title	Salary	Reason for Leaving
Employer: Address:	From: To:			
Employer: Address:	From: To:			
Employer: Address:	From: To:			

If there are any periods of time not accounted for in the Employment Record, please write a brief explanation of what you did during those periods.

_____

_____

ANSWERS AND EXPLANATIONS— READING SKILLS REVIEW

Finding the Main Idea

1. **(B)** is the best answer. The author points out that by seeing someone who had lost a great deal of weight, Cora becomes hopeful that she too could one day be slim. This is the main idea of the story.

Drawing Conclusions

2. **(C)** is the correct answer. Lines 1-8 state that Cora had been trying for years to take off weight, paying no attention to her nagging friend. There is no indication in the passage that she was ever slim.

Finding Supporting Details

3. **(C)** is the correct answer. It is stated in line 29.

Making Inferences About Word Meaning

4. **(A)** is the answer. A job reference is a letter or report on a person's performance from a former employer.

Understanding Figurative Language

5. **(E)** is the best answer. None of the other choices make sense in the context of paragraph one.

Seeing Relationships

6. **(C)** is the best answer. More people are choosing not to have children (lines 9-10) but the passage doesn't say that *most* people are making this choice. Therefore, (A) is false. The passage does not support (B) or (E). (D) is a true statement supported by the passage; however, it doesn't explain why the size of the American family is shrinking. Only (C) can cause family size to shrink.

Finding Supporting Details

7. **(E)** is the correct answer. All of the other choices are listed in the passage as things to think about before choosing a method of birth control.

Finding Supporting Details

8. **(B)** is the correct answer. This fact is stated in lines 44-45. All of the other choices are disproved by the information in the passage.

Following Sequence

9. **(D)** is the correct answer. According to the passage, the best method of birth control can be chosen with the help of a doctor (lines 23-24). If choices (A), (B), (C), or (E) are tried before consulting a doctor, an ineffective or unhealthy method might be chosen.

Seeing Relationships

10. **(A)** A birth control method is effective only if it is used properly. You can therefore conclude that unless personal feelings are considered, the method chosen might be unpleasant to the individual and therefore not be used.

Drawing Conclusions

11. **(D)** is the correct answer. Line 30 states that the pill is not for everyone and should only be used upon a doctor's advice. (A) is too strong a statement to make, based on the information in the passage. There is no evidence for (B) or (E) in the passage. Although (C) is true, it doesn't explain why the pill should be used under a doctor's supervision. The passage does state in lines 42-48 that women with certain health problems cannot use some methods and also that some methods may cause health problems. You can therefore conclude that a doctor's supervision is necessary because the pill may cause health problems.

READING SKILLS REVIEW

Making Inferences About Word Meaning

12. **(C)** is the best answer. The author is showing us a woman who can no longer stand straight because of weariness and pain. Weariness and pain are weighing her down. They are her burdens.

Finding the Main Idea

13. **(B)** is the best answer. The author describes a bowed figure that never lifts its head again, as if there's nothing to look for from life. None of the images in the poem support (A), (C), (D), or (E).

Recognizing Figures of Speech

14. **(D)** is the correct answer. See lines 6-7 and 9-10.

Interpreting Imagery

15. **(D)** is the best answer because autumn is the season in which flowers, trees, and so on, begin to die.

Following Sequence

16. **(E)** is the correct answer. It is stated in line 3.

Understanding Figurative Language

17. **(E)** is the correct answer. In lines 8-11, the author tells us that the four people in gray and white uniforms were ready to serve hundreds of people. In this context, (E) is the only logical answer.

Finding the Main Idea

18. **(A)** is the answer. The story focuses on a woman who feels invisible because she isn't waited on in a restaurant. By speaking up and walking out at the end, she finally feels visible again.

Drawing Conclusions

19. (C) is the correct answer. There is no evidence for (A), (D), or (E) in the passage. (B) is false because lines 6–7 state that there were only about seven other customers in the whole place. In lines 22–23, we see that the waitress thought that the woman had already been served. Therefore, (C) is correct.

Finding Supporting Details

20. (E) is the correct answer. This is described in lines 40–43.

ELMWOOD CENTER FOR HANDICAPPED CHILDREN

139 Chandler Street

Elmwood, Florida

DATE _(today's date)_

NAME _Judy Black_   PHONE _272-5512_

ADDRESS _32 Vista Road, Elmwood, Florida_

POSITION APPLIED FOR _Nurse's Aide_

PERSONAL INFORMATION

SOCIAL SECURITY NUMBER _number applied for_   SINGLE ____ MARRIED ____ OTHER _divorced_

HEIGHT _5'1"_   WEIGHT _102_   NUMBER OF DEPENDENTS _3_   AGES OF DEPENDENTS _4, 6, 7_

DO YOU HAVE ANY PHYSICAL LIMITATIONS?   YES ____   NO ____   (If yes, please specify

No limitations although I have a slight limp.

READING SKILLS REVIEW

HAVE YOU BEEN CONVICTED OF A CRIME WITHIN THE PAST TEN YEARS? YES ____ NO _X_

(If yes, please **furnish details**, as dates, places, offenses, and penalties)

_____

CIRCLE HIGHEST GRADE COMPLETED IN SCHOOL   1 2 3 4 5 6 7 8 9 (10) 11 12 13 14 15 16

NAME OF SCHOOL LAST ATTENDED _Miller High School_   DID YOU GRADUATE? _No_

ADDRESS OF SCHOOL _Elmwood_

HAVE YOU SERVED IN THE ARMED FORCES? YES ____ NO _X_

(If yes, give dates, rank attained, decorations, etc.)

_____

EMPLOYMENT RECORD

Employer and Address	Dates	Job Title	Salary	Reason for Leaving
Employer: City General Hospital Address:	From: 9/74 To: Present	Volunteer Nurse's Aide	None	No Salary
Employer: Address:	From: To:			
Employer: Address:	From: To:			

If there are any periods of time not accounted for in the Employment Record, please write a brief explanation of what you did during those periods.

From June, 1967 to September, 1974, I was taking care of my children.

READING SKILLS REVIEW—EVALUATION CHART

In order to see how well you've done on the Reading Skills Review, see which questions you got right and which ones you got wrong. Then check against the chart below to find out which, if any, types of questions gave you trouble.

Circle the numbers of the questions you got right in the chart below. Enter the number of right answers of each type and the total.

Reading Skill	Question Numbers	Number of Correct Answers	Study Pages
Finding the Main Idea	1, 13, 18		19-26
Finding Supporting Details	3, 7, 8, 20		20-23
Making Inferences About Word Meaning	4, 12		173-181
Following Sequence	9, 16		29-34
Following Directions	Job Application		77-82
Seeing Relationships	6, 10		85-93
Understanding Figurative Language	5, 17		141-150
Interpreting Imagery	15		155-162
Drawing Conclusions	2, 11, 19		127-131
Recognizing Figures of Speech	14		141-144

Total number of correct answers _____

DICTIONARY OF WORDS YOU NEED TO KNOW

abilities — skills; physical or mental powers of performance
> EXAMPLE: A job as a secretary requires certain typing and clerical *abilities*.

acknowledge — to admit knowledge of; to recognize as a fact; to take notice of a fact
> EXAMPLE: You must first *acknowledge* the fact that you can succeed before you take the test.

activated — started in motion; moved into an "on" position; caused to become active
> EXAMPLE: The engineer *activated* the switches, and the train began to move.

agony — great pain in the mind or body
> EXAMPLE: Tony was in *agony* after the car accident.

agreement — having the same opinion; an understanding
> EXAMPLE: The teacher was in complete *agreement* with Bob's interpretation of the story.

ambition — strong hope, wish, or desire; a thing strongly wanted
> EXAMPLE: Glenn had only one *ambition* in life—to make himself happy.

anonymous — giving no name; unknown
> EXAMPLE: The candidate received a large sum of money from an *anonymous* person.

applicant — one who is applying for something (such as a job)
> EXAMPLE: An *applicant* for a position in our factory must fill out two forms.

ashamed — feeling shame; feeling uncomfortable or embarrassed

> EXAMPLE: Some people are *ashamed* to cry in front of others.

autumn — the fall season of the year

> EXAMPLE: I hate to see the leaves on the trees turn brown in *autumn*.

benefit — A. (verb) gain; improve; B. (noun) anything that is of help, that causes a gain or improvement

> EXAMPLE: Do you think the class will *benefit* from reading this book?
> There are many *benefits* that will result from reading that book.

bewildered — confused; puzzled

> EXAMPLE: The city of New York *bewildered* Uncle Kurt when he first came to this country.

bowed — a bending of the body or head out of respect, submission, shame, or pain

> EXAMPLE: Susan *bowed* her head in silent prayer.

capable — being able to do something well; having skill or ability

> EXAMPLE: She was *capable* of doing anything when she wanted to do it badly enough.

census — a counting of the population of a country

> EXAMPLE: According to the most recent *census*, Tokyo has over 9 million people living in the city.

century — each group of one hundred years

> EXAMPLE: The car was invented in the twentieth *century*.

confidence — the quality of being sure of oneself; feeling certain or confident

> EXAMPLE: She gained *confidence* when she got the job.

convenience — freedom from discomfort; ease of use

> EXAMPLE: *Convenience* foods are foods that only need to be heated and served.

cushion — pillow; soft pad

> EXAMPLE: She put a yellow *cushion* on the couch for her head.

delicious — tasting good; enjoyable

> EXAMPLE: The chicken dinner was *delicious*.

dependents — those who rely on another person for support

> EXAMPLE: Sid has three *dependents*—a wife and two children.

depression — very sad feeling; low spirits

> EXAMPLE: Her feeling of *depression* began when she lost her job.

desire — to wish for; to hope for; to long for

> EXAMPLE: I have but one *desire*—to be rich.

destruction — ruin; the act of destroying something; the state of being destroyed

> EXAMPLE: Everywhere you looked, you could see the *destruction* caused by the earthquake.

dimly — faintly; barely able to be seen; not brightly or distinctly

> EXAMPLE: With only one small light bulb to light the room, his room is *dimly* lit.

director — person in charge

> EXAMPLE: The personnel *director* is not taking applications for employment.

discriminate — to make a distinction between two things, persons, or groups; to treat one person or group differently from another

> EXAMPLE: Although it's illegal, some employers still *discriminate* against women.

dispensary — place where medicine is given when needed

> EXAMPLE: The *dispensary* at the army base was located in the main building.

dough — a mixture of flour and other ingredients that is stiff enough to handle

> EXAMPLE: She prepared enough *dough* to make three loaves of fresh bread.

duplicate — an exact copy

> EXAMPLE: The boss likes to have a *duplicate* of every letter he sends out for his files.

echoing — repeating; to hear sound again; ringing

> EXAMPLE: His voice was *echoing* in the hallway.

effectiveness — the state of producing the desired results or effects

> EXAMPLE: The *effectiveness* of her nap was clear to everyone when Mary returned to the living room.

elevator — a device used to lift things or people up and down a multi-storied building

> EXAMPLE: The *elevator* stopped at the third floor, and I stepped out into the hall.

entrance — doorway; a way to come in

> EXAMPLE: The *entrance* to the Adult Learning Center is on Main Street.

experience — know-how; having practice in doing something

> EXAMPLE: Most of his *experience* was in working with a drill press.

expression — a look on one's face

> EXAMPLE: His *expression* instantly changed from happiness to sadness when he learned that this paycheck was his last one.

flare-up — a sudden outburst; a sudden worsening of a situation

> EXAMPLE: I have to go on a strict diet because of a *flare-up* of my old stomach problems.

frail — fragile; weak in body or health

> EXAMPLE: The *frail* woman sitting in the corner is a great-grandmother.

frantically — wildly; excitedly

> EXAMPLE: He looked around *frantically* for the missing child.

hypnotize — to put a person into a condition that seems like sleep, causing the mind to follow directions from another; to create a sleeplike condition in another and have him/her take certain suggestions

> EXAMPLE: Mark *hypnotized* Steve and then told him to act like a dog.

imagine — to form a mental picture of; to use one's imagination

> EXAMPLE: If you can *imagine* what a cross between a moose and a hyena would be like, you've got a good idea of what Sara looks like.

indicated — pointed out

> EXAMPLE: The teacher *indicated* that the test was over.

interview — face-to-face meeting; personal meeting to talk about something

> EXAMPLE: Mr. Smith had his *interview* on Monday and was hired for the job one week later.

learner's permit — a temporary license allowing a person to drive for a certain length of time while learning to drive

 EXAMPLE: Joe got his *learner's permit* last June, and now he's ready to go for his test to get a permanent driver's license.

license — a document that permits a person to do something (a driver's license is required to drive; a marriage license is required before one can get married)

 EXAMPLE: Sam was arrested for driving without a *license*.

limitations — something that causes a person to be limited or restricted

 EXAMPLE: Because of his physical *limitations,* no one wanted to give him a job.

lurching — moving unsteadily; rolling suddenly to one side

 EXAMPLE: I tried to step aside, but the man came *lurching* right toward me.

miracle — unexplained event; highly unusual happening

 EXAMPLE: It was a *miracle* that our team won.

mistake — A. (verb) take the wrong way; B. (noun) error; something wrong

 EXAMPLE: Did you *mistake* the road to Ann's house?
      A *mistake* was made when I paid for the book.

muttered — spoke in a low, unclear tone

 EXAMPLE: "I'm really mad at you," her friend *muttered*.

mysteriously — unknown; not explained

 EXAMPLE: The money was *mysteriously* gone from the table when I returned.

needlepoint — special kind of sewing stitch

 EXAMPLE: Martha made a beautiful *needlepoint* pillow for the couch.

nourishment — food that keeps one in good health

> EXAMPLE: The *nourishment* you give a child is important to his/her growth.

obese — very fat

> EXAMPLE: Diet candy ads always show a picture of an *obese* woman.

ordinary — common, usual

> EXAMPLE: It was an *ordinary* week without any unusual events.

organization — club; organized group of people

> EXAMPLE: The women on my street all belong to the same *organization*.

pelvis — that part of the body located between the hip bones, inside the body

> EXAMPLE: A doctor checks the area of the *pelvis* when he gives a woman her yearly checkup.

perish — to die; to be destroyed

> EXAMPLE: Five people *perished* in the fire.

permit — **A.** (noun) paper allowing a person to perform certain activities; **B.** (verb) to allow; let

> EXAMPLE: Tom Harris had a *permit* to go fishing.
> I did not *permit* Tom to leave the house last night.

persisted — continued in spite of difficulty or opposition

> EXAMPLE: Although I told him six times that my name is Alice, he *persisted* in calling me Susan.

prescribed — ordered the use of something as a remedy or cure

> EXAMPLE: The doctor *prescribed* aspirin and rest for his patients who came down with the flu.

preventive — stopping; an action to stop something from happening

    EXAMPLE: *Preventive* medicine helps people stay well.

prodded — pushed, urged, poked

    EXAMPLE: He was *prodded* into lifting the heavy block of cement.

refused — wouldn't do it; turned it down

    EXAMPLE: The plumber wanted his money when the job was done and *refused* to come back the next day.

regularly — according to the usual method or order; happening again and again

    EXAMPLE: In order to stay in shape, you should exercise *regularly*.

regulations — rules to be followed

    EXAMPLE: The fishing limit was stated in the *regulations*.

rejected — refused to accept or believe

    EXAMPLE: The club *rejected* John's application for membership.

remembered — thought again; recalled; brought back to mind

    EXAMPLE: I *remembered* to buy milk and bread on the way home from work.

requirements — those things that are necessary to do or have

    EXAMPLE: The *requirements* of the job included being able to type and to answer the telephone.

responsibility — duty; being in charge; a job that one must do

    EXAMPLE: He had the *responsibility* of answering the office telephone.

retain — to keep; hold onto

    EXAMPLE: The thin woman has a problem trying to *retain* weight.

revoked — canceled; abolished

    EXAMPLE: Bob's driver's license was *revoked* after he got his third speeding ticket in six months.

sensation — feeling; excitement of the senses

    EXAMPLE: It was quite a *sensation* to jump into the cold lake after walking in the hot sun for two hours.

severely — harshly; very seriously

    EXAMPLE: The woman spoke *severely* to her child after he had run out in traffic to get his baseball.

shrinkage — the act of getting smaller

    EXAMPLE: The *shrinkage* in the yarn was caused by washing the sweater in hot water.

slouched — bent over; sagging

    EXAMPLE: Alan was *slouched* over the table.

society — a group of people

    EXAMPLE: In today's *society,* some people need to work two jobs to make ends meet.

sponsor — someone who takes responsibility for some other person or thing

    EXAMPLE: You don't need a *sponsor* to join this class. You can come on your own.

struggle — try very hard against opposition; fight

    EXAMPLE: The wounded horse tried to *struggle* to its feet, but it was too late.

suffice — meet the needs of; to provide

    EXAMPLE: I don't need much money. Ten dollars will *suffice.*

supervision — direction; the act of overseeing and directing something or someone

    EXAMPLE: Some people work better without constant *supervision.*

surgery — that part of medicine involving cutting the patient

    EXAMPLE: She had *surgery* to fix her back when she was unable to walk.

suspended — took away a privilege for a temporary period of time; to withhold something temporarily as punishment

    EXAMPLE: His right to drive the company car was *suspended* when the police caught him driving without a license.

throbbing — vibrating; beating like a drum

    EXAMPLE: Jim's head was *throbbing* when he woke up in the morning.

trend — style; direction

    EXAMPLE: The new *trend* in clothing is toward longer skirts again.

twang — sharp ringing sound; nasal tone of voice

    EXAMPLE: The *twang* of the guitar could be heard in the next room.

unconscious — not aware; temporarily deprived of consciousness or awareness

    EXAMPLE: She hit her head on the door and was *unconscious* for about two minutes.

vary — change in form or nature

    EXAMPLE: The quality of his work may *vary*, depending on his mood.

vital — essential, necessary

    EXAMPLE: It's *vital* that you finish typing up that report before the meeting.

vehicle — a conveyance; something with wheels or runners used for carrying other things

    EXAMPLE: His 1953 Dodge was the most broken-down *vehicle* that I had ever seen.

volunteer — A. (noun) one who gives time without charge; free help; B. (verb) to help without getting paid; offer

    EXAMPLE: The *volunteer* worked in the hospital every Tuesday.
    Did you *volunteer* to help at the party?

weariness — fatigue; state of being extremely tired

    EXAMPLE: After having argued for the past two hours, both people now spoke with *weariness* rather than anger.